I've Been Rich.
I've Been Poor.
Rich Is Better.

I've Been Rich.
I've Been Poor.
Rich Is Better.

Judy Resnick

with Gene Stone

Golden Books

New York

Golden Books®

888 Seventh Avenue
New York, NY 10106

This book is based on the author's research and expertise in the field of investment
and retirement planning. Like all books on this subject matter, it is not a substitute for
financial advice. Consult a financial adviser prior to making substantial investments.
To protect the privacy of individuals in this book, certain names, places, and other
identifying facts have been changed.

Golden Books® and colophon
are trademarks of Golden Books Publishing Co., Inc.
Designed by Suzanne Noli
Manufactured in the United States of America

10   9   8   7   6   5   4   3   2   1

Library of Congress Cataloging-in-Publication Data
Resnick, Judy.
    I've Been Rich. I've Been Poor. Rich Is Better. /
Judy Resnick with Gene Stone.
        p.   cm.
    Includes index.
    ISBN 0-307-44005-2
    1. Women—Finance, Personal.   2. Investments.   3. Finance,
Personal.   I. Stone, Gene W.   II. Title.
HG179.R394   1998
332.024′042—dc21   97-25527
                                                    CIP

To my daughters, Audrey and Stacey. It was because of you that the notion of giving up was always unthinkable. Nothing in my life has meant more than seeing you both grow into wise and wonderful women. I love you so very much.

Acknowledgments

So many generous people have helped me along the way that there isn't room to list them all, but I do want to give special thanks to the following: Jesse Kornbluth, Peter Lewis, Chris Malzone, Lynda Resnick, Stuart Snyder, and Marjorie Wallace.

Many other people contributed to the writing of the book. For help on the topics of financial planning and investing, I'm indebted to Gail Kamer, Agnes Mura, and Terry Hamacher; on taxes, Bob Shuwarger, Mark Kornspan, Mike Merlis, and Edward J. Mahoney; on estate planning, Sarah Greenlee Rubin and Paul J. Livadary; on insurance, Nathan Greenlee, Dave Ford, and Elizabeth Sampson. Nathan Greenlee was also invaluable in working out many of the book's retirement formulas.

I'd also like to thank my agent, Jan Miller, as well as my editor at Golden Books, Bob Asahina, and my copy editor, Miranda Spencer.

Contents

I'm on My Own, and So Are You

I've been rich and I've been poor. Rich is better.

Sophie Tucker

$\mathcal{N}$ot long ago a 39-year-old free-lance writer whom I'll call Melissa met me for a quick lunch. Melissa, divorced with one daughter, receives child support from the father, but he barely earns enough money to take care of his new family. And although she's talented, Melissa seldom makes more than $25,000 a year. She does have a boyfriend who's been unusually generous, but he hasn't been giving off any marriage signals.

A month before we met, Melissa's uncle died, and she discovered, to her surprise, that he'd left her $250,000.

"What are you going to do with all that money?" I asked.

"I've always wanted to buy a house," Melissa said. "It's been my dream ever since the divorce. . . ." She talked about the splendor of houses for another few minutes.

When she paused long enough to look at me, I returned her gaze squarely and said, "That's insane."

Melissa wasn't expecting a frontal attack. She gulped.

"That's the wrong move," I continued. "Do you want to end up broke someday, living on the street?" I hate being subtle.

"What's wrong with a house?" Melissa asked.

I explained. Here she was, lucky enough to land $250,000 out of the blue. What should she do with it? Invest it. But not in one piece of real estate. Sure, everyone wants a home. But should Melissa put all of her money into a single investment? Absolutely, positively not.

"I hate renting," Melissa insisted. "I want my own place."

"Of course you do," I replied. "But that doesn't mean that you can afford to buy one."

A wet drop formed in Melissa's right eye. Still I was determined to make her listen, no matter how teary she became. I'm as emotional as anyone, but I learned a long time ago that feelings can interfere with common sense.

"I'm still young," Melissa said. "Anything can happen."

By that she meant, as I learned after ten more minutes of conversation, that she could still find a man to take care of her.

"Maybe," I said. "But more likely, you won't."

Another tear formed, now in her left eye. Melissa was good. But I had done this too many times before. I must have talked to Melissa for a full hour. "Don't put all your eggs in one basket," I explained. "Be sensible. This isn't the moment to surrender to dreams. If you take that inheritance and spread it around carefully into many different investments, you'll probably never lose it. If you put it all into one piece of property, your risk is much greater. In your financial position, a home is a luxury."

Melissa's resolve was weakening.

"This is a golden opportunity," I continued. "Don't blow it. Lock this money into investments that will give you some real growth over time. Then leave them alone.

"It appears that you're the only one you can count on now. So you have to assume no one else will be there when you're older, either."

At that moment the tears in Melissa's eyes burst the dam of her resolve and flowed down her cheeks. She sat still and silent, hands on her forehead, ignoring her blackened catfish salad.

I wasn't trying to hurt her. All I was trying to do was help her take care of herself, realistically.

When she was ready to talk again, we discussed her future at length. When we were done, the tears had dried, although the catfish remained uneaten.

"You're right," she said. "You really are."

Instead of buying the house, Melissa, who turned out to be a good listener, invested the money carefully. Today she's making almost as much from her portfolio as she earns from writing. She's living well and she's growing her money.

The waiters at my favorite restaurants are used to taking away my friends' plates even when they're still filled with food. It's hard to eat and face the reality of money all at once.

◆ ◆ ◆

Here's another story, this one concerning Monica, a beautiful 69-year-old. Monica walked into my office calmly and asked for an espresso, which she sipped deliberately for a full five minutes before she, too, burst into tears. (Not that all women cry when they talk about money, but many of the most dramatic incidents in our lives tend to be unhappy ones. Anyway, sometimes it takes courage to cry openly.)

Monica's story soon became clear. She had spent her entire life looking for the right man, because she had been taught from childhood that The Male thinks about The Money and The Female thinks about The Home. "I always knew that Prince Charming was going to arrive one day and save me," she said.

"And did he?" I asked.

"Several men *seemed* to be Prince Charming," she replied. But each one turned out to be the Prince of Darkness. Monica had been married twice. Her first husband was a handsome ne'er-do-well who left her flat and dry. After a few years of searching frantically for the next husband, Monica found herself an older, wealthy businessman and stayed married to him for ten years, until he left her for a younger woman. However, this time Monica received a more appropriate settlement of $1.5 million.

She never bothered to focus on her money, however. Instead, Monica's only financial plan was to find still another man. Unfortunately, she failed.

Worse, she surrendered responsibility of her money to a broker whom she'd selected only because they had a friend in common.

Without looking into his credentials, she handed the man her entire account, and within months he'd lost a great deal of the money by betting too heavily on precarious investments. He wasn't dishonest. He just wasn't smart.

After it was too late, Monica sued him, but she lost the case. His lawyers successfully argued that Monica knew what she was doing when she gave the man full discretion. She should have done her homework before handing over her money.

Monica then took her remaining assets and moved them into mutual funds. Unfortunately, this was 1994, which was a bad year for the market, so to cut her losses, she pulled her money out once again, and this time placed it with another, more qualified broker. If she'd stayed put in the mutual funds, however, she would have done fine, as 1995 and 1996 were excellent years for most mutual funds. Instead, she had to pay additional commissions and had less to invest each year.

Monica owned her condo as well as a small house that she rented out, and had $300,000 in cash. She'd been spending more than $90,000 a year on expenses. It was clear that something had to give. At least, it was clear to me.

"Even if you cut your expenses by $25,000," I said, "you can't make it work."

"What can I do?" she asked.

I told her to change her life-style: Sell her home, invest the cash, and rent something cheaper. Monica could live another thirty years, and she didn't intend to earn any more money. We had to create enough income to support her (which we tried to do: see page 180).

Over the years I've seen many women who've focused on a man as their sole source of financial support end up in a bad place. As I told Monica, the real lesson here isn't just about money, but independence. Monica never thought she'd have to support herself because she was so attractive.

Even when our meeting was over and the crying had stopped, she admitted, "I'm still looking for a man. Isn't every woman?"

"Many of us are indeed looking for men," I said, "but the smart ones are looking for a warm, caring relationship rather than life support."

◆ ◆ ◆

Here are a few facts of life that women are just beginning to figure out:

- Prince Charming hit the road sometime back in the 1950s.
- The world of business isn't a fair place.
- Total dependence on others can be dangerous to your health and your wealth.
- Only you are responsible for your own financial security.

It's not that the times are changing. The times have already changed. Women no longer spend all their lives at home. Men no longer go out and make all the money.

The bottom line is that there isn't a single person out there who can truly guarantee any woman financial security—except herself. This means that if you're married, you must educate yourself financially, even if your partner is making money for both of you. If you're living with someone, you must do the same. And if you're earning your own money, you still have to educate yourself, because your paycheck supports you only today—it's what you save and invest that supports you tomorrow. Ignoring this reality doesn't work—not if you want to end up self-sufficient and secure; not if you want to avoid wearing rags and pushing a shopping cart down the block.

Hear me again. There is one basic economic fact of life with which you must come to terms: You, and only you, are responsible for your own economic survival.

That's right. Not your husband. Not your business partner. Not your father. Not your family. You. So if you haven't already done so, it's time to get your economic act together and take charge of your money.

But alongside these dire warnings comes some good news: I can help you learn to take care of your finances. I can teach you how to feel more secure. I can help you put aside your fears about the subject of money.

I can help because I had to learn how to take care of myself the hard way—all by myself. It was a tough, sad, and lonely road. But this is part of what makes my information valuable. As a friend said to me, "Judy, you have an incredible, painful story. So do a lot of other women. The difference is that yours has a positive result."

After all, as you will see, I went from losing my health, my money, and most of my adult family to becoming a highly successful entrepreneur. And the best part of my story isn't all the money I've made, the car I drive, or the presents I can buy. The best part is that I can wake up every morning, look at myself in the mirror, and be totally confident that I know how to take care of those whom I love the most, including myself.

◆ ◆ ◆

How do you know if you're taking good care of your own wealth? For starters, ask yourself these questions:

- Do I have enough money if I get divorced or lose my significant other?
- Do I have enough money if I become sick or disabled?
- Do I have enough money if I lose my job or my earnings drop?
- Do I have enough money if I decide to start my own business?
- Do I have enough money to retire?
- Do I take care of my money as I would any other major responsibility in my life?

You probably answered "no" or "I don't know" to at least some, if not all, of these questions. Most women do, and there's nothing to be ashamed of. That's just the way it's always been. Too many women aren't ready to make important financial decisions, or they fail to understand the consequences of the decisions they've already made—

or that were made for them. In my case, I was over 40 before I paid any attention to these decisions. Until then the men in my life made every one of them for me.

But it doesn't have to be this way.

The women's movement helped so many of us break through barriers that once seemed impenetrable. Years ago, when my ex-husband told me to stay at home and clean, I obeyed him without a whimper. Today, I'd tell him that we should hire a housekeeper because I work as hard as he does. Harder, actually. My father used to say, "Judy, you're so smart, I only wish you'd been a son." He meant it as a compliment. If he were alive today, I'd ask him to show me his profit and loss statement so I could help him manage his affairs more efficiently.

Nowadays women are mothers and merchants, homemakers and heart surgeons, daughters and dentists, executive's wives and executives. Many of us are juggling dual roles. We have more money, we're working longer, we're living longer. There are more than ten million executive, senior-level management and professional women in the United States. Women own 40 percent of all retail and service companies, as well as 30 percent of all domestic businesses—more than eight million companies altogether, or one-third of all American firms. That number is growing at double the rate of firms owned by men. Those eight million businesses employ one-third more employees than all the Fortune 500 companies put together.

Female executive compensation has increased by 18.3 percent since 1993, compared with 1.7 percent for male executives. From 1982 to 1992, the number of female executive vice presidents doubled. Some 43 percent of all Americans with gross assets of $500,000 or more are women. Women constitute 35 percent of the country's 51 million owners of stocks and stock mutual funds.

But if we've become experts at doing everything that's expected of us and more, we still haven't fully penetrated the world of finance, nor have we learned how to build our net worth. That fact continued to gnaw at me, even as my own career prospered. I was burning with ambition to do more. I didn't know exactly what direction that would take, however, until two years ago, when my friend Stuart asked me if I would talk to his friend Maureen, who was suffering from terrible financial advice.

It turned out that Maureen had been married to an extremely unpleasant man who was so manipulative that, although dead, he was still controlling her. After their divorce, this husband had arranged their settlement in such a way that whenever Maureen needed money, she had to petition a trust for funds. And after he died, the estate was left in charge of the money, rather than his ex-wife. The estate trustees' brokers placed Maureen's money into mutual funds, and although the funds were decent, they didn't serve her purpose, because the brokerage firm never took the time to read the trust agreements. The husband had tied things up so that Maureen was allowed to withdraw only interest income—she wasn't permitted to take out any capital gains or dividends (which we'll define later). Since the mutual funds paid only dividends, she wasn't even earning interest, the one thing she really needed.

Thanks to someone else's incompetence, Maureen became a cash-poor millionaire.

I told her all this and, with a little work and a long conversation with her trustees, we were able to establish a better portfolio. But the situation infuriated me. "Look at how badly women get treated," I told my business partner, Neil Dabney.

Neil shrugged his shoulders. "That's just life."

"It's easy for a man to say that," I retorted, "because it's not a man's thing. It's women who are always being set up for this kind of predicament."

I couldn't stop. "That brokerage firm saw big commissions when they saw Maureen. Those guys didn't bother to do their homework. If they had ever read her trust, they would have known what to do, but did they? No!"

I had worked myself into a frenzy. "I should be doing something about this," I said. "Now!"

And that was my moment of inspiration. *I'm supposed to do this!* I thought. Everything happens for a reason. This was what my ambition burned for: not for some higher paying, more powerful job, but one that could help women learn from what I learned, one that could set them on the course to financial independence.

What I finally realized—after I'd repeated myself so often that poor Neil wondered if I'd turned into a broken record—was that I was looking to achieve something very similar to what I'd been seeking from my personal psychotherapy. I once told my psychiatrist, "Help me find a way to make something positive from all the losses I've endured in my life, so that they don't destroy me." And he did.

Now, sixteen years later, I was staring in the face of that idea again: trying to make something positive of everything—good and bad—that I'd endured in life since that time, beginning with my first job all the way to starting my own company. I knew if I could use my experiences to teach other women what I'd learned about financial accumulation and markets, and along the way I could also demystify the deep, dark secret world of money, I would indeed be making something positive out of all my life events.

◆ ◆ ◆

Once I'd realized my mission, my basic concept was to wake women up to the reality of finance. Three agendas lay within that concept. The first was to make women more aware of what risk really means when it comes to investing money. The second was to teach women to become financially independent and not to rely on men, or anyone else, to make all their financial decisions. The third was to encourage women to be willing to educate themselves, and to become proud of their knowledge of finance.

Let's talk about **risk** first.

What is risk in the financial world? It's something you run into the very minute you take your money out of a bank (the world of guaranteed safety), in order to invest it in other assets, such as bonds or stocks.

But it's a much bigger risk to avoid risk entirely. Without risk, you simply can't enjoy financial growth, and without growth, you're at risk for the rest of your life.

Not all risk is equal. There is crazy, silly risk, and there is calculated, educated risk. I believe only in the latter. And believe me, I've seen both types.

So often women resist the idea of investing their money outside the safe world of certificates of deposit (CDs). And for a good reason: Historically, women haven't been risk takers. We've been gaining new earning power and controlling more assets, but many of us still tend to keep our money in the proverbial pillowcase—out of fear of losing that money. Men, however, have always been willing to invest, which is why they've controlled most of the money. Their jobs have always meant going out into the world and taking risks, while women remained sheltered at home. Only now are women learning about taking risks as they become commercial pilots, surgeons, army sergeants, or any other job once considered off-limits to females.

Yet, if you think about it, there is one risk that women have been taking for years, and that's whom they choose to marry. That's right: A husband has traditionally been a woman's biggest risk. You don't think you're taking a risk when you marry? How safe is it to say, "I'm not going to learn about money, I'm going to bet my entire financial life on this one guy"? As my gambling-loving father would have said, this is called placing all your chips on one number. Look at the odds —there's a 50 percent divorce rate in our country!

Still, the risk that women normally tell me they fear is taking their money away from some "safe" place, like under the mattress, and putting it in the markets. It's time to overcome this fear, just as women are overcoming their fear in so many other areas. Later in this book I'll show you how to do it.

The willingness to take prudent risks is necessary to any investment strategy. So what if historically women haven't been risk takers? History always changes. It's changing right now.

◆ ◆ ◆

Now let's talk about **financial independence,** or why it's not a good idea to depend on men, or anyone else, to make all your financial decisions.

Mind you, I'd never recommend you work only with women. That wouldn't make any sense. But in order to plan your financial life intelligently, you must feel free to talk as frankly as possible with your financial adviser. How can you, if you're afraid to tell your adviser that you've put your savings into a CD at a neighborhood bank because you feel comfortable there, but you can't really explain why?

Over the years women have tended to be more open than men when dealing with emotional issues. You'd probably be likely to share your financial fears if the person sitting across the desk was equally willing to part with his. But most men aren't as candid about their emotional lives as women.

Personally, whenever I'm working on my financial matters, I feel it's an absolute necessity to open up. I want to feel free to talk about my needs for the future, my fears, my family, and my friends. To do that, I like to discuss these issues honestly, with the kind of detail that makes it possible to address all my concerns. So when I have my money managed, I want someone interested not just in my money, but in me.

And as a financial adviser, I encourage my clients to be equally honest and forthright. One reason so many women are candid with me is because of my full-disclosure policy. I'm not some suit behind a desk. I don't have a lot of secrets. I don't believe in them. The only secrets I keep are other people's, for if someone shares an intimate piece of knowledge about her life and asks me not to reveal it, my lips are sealed. But my own life? It's an open book, literally, all 205 pages of it.

I think that most other women want to be frank about their lives, too, and given the encouragement, they will be.

Women tend to be more emotionally open because they understand their lives are holistic. How a person spends money has to do with her psyche as much as her budget. For instance, compulsive spenders may be buying too many clothes to make themselves feel whole; the issue's root cause is emotional, not financial. It's easier to say that sort of a thing to a woman than a man. Men have similar issues, but try telling a man that he should talk to a psychologist about his spending problems. I have. He doesn't want to hear it.

Men usually separate their finances from their emotions. I've yet to hear a man tell me about his despair when talking about his money. I'm still waiting for a man to cry. And believe me, considering what some men have done to their finances, many should be in tears. But men separate the issues; they put up a wall, they compartmentalize their lives. "I'm here to talk money," they say. "My money is my money, my kids are my kids, my depression is my depression." Period. Try arguing with that. Better to argue with a brick wall.

I see all those things—money, kids, family, emotions—as elements of the same thing. You. Your life, your money, your heart, are all a part of you. When you're talking about your money, you're talking about a part of your life's blood, along with your health, family, friends, spirituality. Can you imagine visiting your doctor and not admitting that you've been feeling a strange pain in your back? Yet so many women have told me that when they see their brokers, they're afraid to confess their ignorance of certain issues and remain silent until they return home, when they curse themselves for not having spoken up. They're afraid to say, "My friend is earning ten percent, and I'm only earning five. Why?" I've known many a woman who claims that her financial adviser will lean over and say, "You can't take that kind of risk," and then start talking to her as if he were her father. That's not a good professional relationship.

As I said, don't avoid male advisers. Many of my closest consultants and coworkers are men. My former business partner is a man. My favorite estate lawyer is a man. The person writing this book with me is a man. I'm simply saying that you shouldn't let someone make decisions for you without some form of involvement on your part. So if your financial adviser isn't giving you the kind of openness and communication you need, demand it. If that doesn't work, make a change. Remember, it's your money and it's your life.

The need to educate yourself is also extremely important. Over the years men have evolved financially, and women haven't. Men have always controlled the money, and women haven't. Men have always built their net worth, and women haven't. And men start young, too. At his bar mitzvah, when my cousin Stewart was asked what he wanted to be when he grew up, he replied, "Rich." (And today he certainly is.) I would have said, "Married, with children." (As I once was.)

But things have changed, and if you don't educate yourself at least a little about money, you may find yourself in trouble. Now, for years women were afraid to accumulate or show off this kind of knowledge, for if we seemed overly capable and strong, no one (i.e., no male) would come along to take care of us. But I can vouch that the odds of someone taking care of you permanently are low. If there ever was a White Knight, he's probably knee-deep in alimony by now (and his gallant steed is long dead). The era of handing responsibility for your life over to a man has ended, and more and more women understand that, like it or not, it's their own knowledge that's going to help them prosper. So go ahead, be proud of your knowledge—particularly if what you're showing off is how responsible you are for your own future.

I know if women would only own up to their responsibility for their financial knowledge, they, too, would be able to build their own wealth. Women can understand how money works, and we have— when we've taken the trouble to learn. There are some wonderful examples of women who, once they took the time to educate themselves, have become successful and wealthy in their own right. Perhaps no one expected these women to understand money either, but they didn't care. They learned what they needed to know, and once they did, there was no stopping them.

◆ ◆ ◆

There was no stopping me, either. I quickly looked up Gail Kamer, an old friend and a financial planner who had retired a few years earlier and was now sitting around her house, knitting one sweater after another. (It was making me crazy. She has only one grandson. How many sweaters can that child wear? He had to be the warmest boy in Beverly Hills.)

"At least knit some sweaters for my grandkids," I said, "or better, help me get this message out."

Gail listened to what I had to say and put down her knitting needles. "I'll do it," she said.

We decided the best approach was to organize three dinners for women who wanted to learn about money, each one to be set up similarly: First, I would introduce myself, talk about my life and how I came to be giving these meetings, and then we would present a short seminar on personal finance and investing. I also hoped that, during the evening, some of the women might tell their own stories, too.

In September 1995 I sent out invitations to a mailing list of women with businesses in Beverly Hills, hoping against hope that maybe a dozen would attend. I didn't know most of the women we invited; I did know they were enormously busy.

As is often the case, the unexpected happened. None of us could ever have guessed that the room would be overflowing with respondents: businesswomen, divorced women, widowed women, rich women, poor women, even a mother and daughter who didn't know the other was coming. All the participants were delighted to be present and they reached a quick consensus: We have good jobs, they said, or we have good husbands, or we have good money, or we have good prospects. But that's not enough, they admitted. We've never taken responsibility for that money. It's time we do so.

Each dinner proceeded as planned. First, I introduced myself as the CEO of Dabney/Resnick, the mother of Audrey and Stacey, and the grandmother of Jake, Jessica, and Benjamin (Keaton, my youngest grandchild, hadn't been born yet). We then went around the table, each woman introducing herself as she saw fit: Some discussed their businesses, some their families, and many both. Next, after I told my story, the audience opened up their own lives and spoke of wonderful marriages, horrendous divorces, happy families, unpleasant relationships—the range was extraordinary, and the process couldn't have been more lovely. By the end of each evening many of us were close to tears, as the stories were often deeply moving. By now we weren't talking only about finance, but about independence, too, and how terrific it would feel to face the world knowing you had the freedom to do whatever you wished.

What we eventually discovered was that each woman present shared some form of the same nightmare: sliding into financial ruin. As you'll soon see, it happened to me. It had happened to a few of the women in the room. And it was something that each and every one of them feared.

And yet, also like myself years ago, very few of these women had taken good care of their financial lives, and I realized that I was dealing with a big black hole. Right there I began formulating a business plan. I wanted to help these women get their money into the best possible shape, and help them learn how to take responsibility by understanding how to protect and grow their assets in the future.

In 1996 I formed The Resnick Group, Inc., to manage women's money, and more: Part of our goal is and always will be to educate. How different would we be from any other program if all we did was take the money and leave the woman in financial darkness? We don't force anyone to learn any more than she wants, but we do encourage our clients to become as involved as they comfortably can. Some are still shy, and some are afraid to learn, but others are actively trying to understand a field that only a few years ago was a completely blank screen.

The bottom line is that all women should feel free to make any life choice they wish—so they can get married, and stay married, out of love rather than need; so they can be motivated by enlightened self-interest, rather than by fear. It's time to put fear aside, overcome inertia, roll up our sleeves, and get to work. It's time we learn how to be responsible for our money, just as we have learned to be responsible for our minds, our bodies, our health, and our spirituality.

Today I'm working with a fast-growing circle of women of all ages and income levels. But this isn't enough. If so many women in Los Angeles heard and responded to my message, how many must there be in the rest of the country? My next goal was to reach as many of these women as possible, so I sat down with several advisers, mulled it over, and decided that the best strategy was to write a book. And you're reading that book right now.

Growing Up, and Financial Independence

What I know about money, I learned the
hard way—by having had it.
Margaret Halsey

*W*henever a new client comes to The Resnick Group, one of the first items we discuss is a **budget.** Although it's not essential for every woman, I recommend at least considering one. Here we stress the importance of savings and preserving what you already have, which is the core of the story. If you don't save, you won't have anything to invest. Until I reached my forties I never knew how to save; I only knew how to spend. I wasn't able to become financially secure until I learned to accumulate cash, so there was something left over to invest.

Next, we discuss the five essential elements of the financial planning process.

First is **tax planning,** which is something you must attend to each and every year. Remember, one dollar earned isn't the same as one dollar after taxes. Many women I've worked with forget about taxes when they prepare their budgets. Also, it's important to know how to use ethical professionals for your tax preparation. And most of all, are you yourself honest when you fill out your taxes? You'd better be.

Estate planning sounds gloomy, but it's an absolute necessity. As a friend once said, estate planning isn't about dying, it's about planning for the future. Are you well prepared for your own death? It may not be something you want to think about today, but it's something you must do. Have you consulted a lawyer about your will? If you're married, has your husband prepared a will or trust? What about your mother and father—have they taken care of their estate plan sensibly? You can help them if they haven't, and save yourself a lot of money in taxes in the future as well. Have you thought about what happens to your own children? Are there certain charities you care for? It's not difficult to help them, and yourself too, in your will.

Insurance planning is designed to protect what you already have. This includes medical, disability, auto, and health insurance, as well as professional and personal liability. Do you know what an umbrella policy is? Half the women I talk to don't have a clue about the importance of good coverage. What about long-term care? Have you thought about what will happen to you when you reach 65? Do you really think Medicare will be enough to cover your needs? One of my primary goals is to make sure that every woman learns to be properly insured throughout her entire life, whether she's married or single, widowed or divorced, childless or the mother of ten.

My own specialty is **investment planning.** Once everything else is in place, and you understand how much money you need for all of the above, you can set up an investment program to earn top dollar from what's left over. Do you know the difference between a large cap and a small cap stock? Do you know the difference between a stock and a bond? A no-load fund and a front-load fund? A broker and a money manager? Read on.

What could sound easier than **retirement planning?** You'll want to retain your present life-style after you stop working. That seems simple enough. Then why do so few women prepare for retirement adequately? How do you know if you have enough set aside for life after you stop working? I can't tell you how many women aren't ready to retire. At my firm we request that every woman, whether she's 25 or 60, consider her future as though it were today. Because what you do today affects every moment of your future.

By the time you've finished this book, you'll not only understand more about each of the above elements involved in financial planning, you'll be ready to put them into practice.

You're luckier than I was. At least someone is raising these issues for you. I had to find out all of the above for myself, and in the worst way possible. I had to discover that my Prince Charming was an illusion, as well as lose most of my family and almost all of my money. I had to learn that being dependent and having no financial knowledge is devastating. But no one's life is entirely good or bad. With each setback came the opportunity to experience growth. The only reason I can claim to understand financial realities today is that the events of my life conspired to ensure that I did. For me, it was a matter of pure survival.

It all started back in the 1940s in suburban New Jersey, where I grew up thinking that the world was going to treat me as its special little girl and take care of me forever. Isn't that what men are supposed to do for women? I come from a long line of females who were brought up to please males. And they were damn good at it.

My parents met when they were teenagers. She was Frances Silverstein, he was Louis Resnick, and they both lived in New York City. Frances was a first-generation American with three sisters and two brothers in a family that was so poor they stood in line for food and clothes. Because her family needed the money, my mother had to drop out of high school to work. Grandpa Benjamin was a lovable, sweet man, but not much of a provider. When she saw him in his coffin at his funeral, dressed up in his one good suit as though he had finally landed a well-paying job, my grandmother Sophie sighed and told his corpse that he never looked so good.

Fran found this poverty deeply troubling, and she knew in her heart of hearts that, someday, she was going to find a man to provide for her. Lou Resnick was that man.

Lou's father William had emigrated from Russia, purchasing a passport with the name Resnick on it so he could get out of the country; thus was a world of American Resnicks born. Grandfather William alternately bullied his kids and ignored his wife. At my grandmother

Ida's funeral, my mother told me that no matter what illness was listed on her death certificate, Ida had really died of neglect.

When Fran met Lou she was making a measly living selling fabric. She took a close look at this bright, attractive man, and what she saw was a solid provider. The world had smiled on Fran, and soon she was married. She was 20 years old; Lou was 22 and driving a coffee delivery truck.

Lou's first gift to Fran was curtains for her parents' apartment. More than a kiss ever could, that gesture solidified and characterized their relationship. Lou was a caretaker, not just for her, but for her entire family.

A few years later, the couple moved to Livingston, New Jersey, where, in 1938, my older brother, Gary, was born. Soon they moved once more—my father was a serial mover, constantly upgrading his environment in that only-in-America way, taking us someplace new every time he felt he could afford more.

I was born December 2, 1941, five days before the bombing of Pearl Harbor, a fact that my father never grew tired of telling his friends. Soon afterward Lou moved us to New Brunswick, in the first house I can remember, and in 1946 my younger sister, Roni, was born. The late 1940s were a prosperous time and Lou's career, fueled by hard work and earnest intentions, flourished. Soon he had transferred over to what at the time was called "the refrigeration business," a polite way of saying that he sold large appliances. Lou owned his own business, made good money, and gave Fran the life of her dreams. The marriage was good. Life was good. Mom stayed home, Dad went to work, and the family was close, filled with loving cousins and relatives. The only glitch in our lives was a sudden move to Arizona, where we lived for fourteen months. Why this happened remains a family mystery, but my mother didn't complain. We just packed up and moved, and then, moved back.

I felt so sophisticated. No one else in my class had ever flown on an airplane, and here I was, returning from a sojourn out west. For show-and-tell I brought in a cactus and told all my friends about life on the other side of the world.

Up until this point, like most girls at my age, these friends were other girls. Now, as I entered the fifth grade, the opposite sex, once completely insignificant, began to take on an air of both distant mystery and pressing importance.

Every Wednesday evening throughout the year I'd been attending a children's dance program, and I loved dancing, especially with Louis, the cutest boy in the class.

Back then my nicest feature was my long, dark hair, which Louis always complimented. Then, one afternoon after school, my mom took a hard look at me, sat me down on a stool, and the next thing I knew, with a few quick snips of the scissors, she had cut my life into shreds. My hair! Most of it was lying on the floor, the rest hanging in a chin-length bob around my head.

At the dance that night, the moment the music started, all dressed up in my pink dress and my new short hairdo, I searched the room for Louis. When I spotted him I walked tentatively in his direction until he saw me, and took a couple of steps forward. The expression on his face as he examined my head—something between shock and disdain—was terrifying. He edged closer, trying to make sure his eyes weren't deceiving him, and then he turned and walked away. A moment later he was dancing with Sarabeth Wortheimer.

I knew exactly what this meant. My hair was horrible. I'd learned my first lesson. If you want to attract boys, please them. The flip side of the lesson was, don't please your mother. If it weren't for her, I'd be dancing with Louis.

From this point on I could feel a subtle push by everyone around me to make myself appealing to males—particularly from that very person who had just made me so unappealing—my mother. With her help I started figuring out all those things that it took to attract guys. And what things! Consciously or unconsciously, it didn't take me long to understand. It was all about working their egos. Girls had to make boys feel that they were smarter, that they could run faster, that they could jump higher—anything we could do, they could do better.

On top of that, we had to look good, too.

The situation isn't as bad today as it was in the '40s and '50s, because girls now receive more encouragement to compete with boys. Yet I still run into many young women who say that when the chips are down, they feel they must let the male think he's won. This certainly seems true in business. I have many male peers and friends, but plenty of times I can see that they'd be a good deal happier if I knew a good deal less. But I don't want to know less. Not anymore.

◆ ◆ ◆

Just as it seemed as though our family was settling into New Jersey for good, in 1952 my father announced that we were moving to Southern California.

My mother broke down. Her entire family lived in Brooklyn. A brief stop in Arizona had been tolerable, but California? My mother retreated to the bedroom in tears. But she couldn't say no. Lou had agreed to provide for her, and he was keeping up his end of the bargain. He just never said where he was going to provide. And my mother didn't believe in rocking the boat. Her motto was, "Never leave your husband's bed." Another motto was, "Don't draw a line in the sand for your man." My mother had many mottoes, but they all amounted to one thing: Compliance.

She did what was necessary. My brother and father drove across the country and found a nice house in Long Beach, and three weeks later my mother, my sister, and I were flown in to join them. At least they didn't make us take a covered wagon.

My mother accepted the new circumstances, but she didn't calm down. Discreetly, she sniffled and sighed, making sure that Lou heard every little moan. What was a man to do? In my father's case, the answer was to move her mother, father, and even her brother, bachelor Uncle Leon, out west to live in our house.

My father was now making a good living running liquor stores. And I was sent off to Will Rogers Junior High. For me, the move was a dream come true. California in the 1950s was a children's paradise—

the beach, rock 'n' roll, the sun. It was Surf City, USA, as painted by Norman Rockwell. I loved our new home, the beach, my parents, my siblings. I loved my life.

◆ ◆ ◆

In 1953, when I was 11 years old, I became quite sick. It started on a family outing to Knott's Berry Farm, when my mother, noticing that I was flushed and warm, insisted we go home. But the temperature kept recurring, along with facial puffiness and a general sense of discomfort, and so she took me to see a doctor, whose diagnosis was serious: acute glomerulonephritis, or a kidney disorder. I had to remain in bed for at least the next seven months.

My mother didn't handle my illness well. One of her friends had just lost a child, and she was terrified that I was next. One night I heard her crying through my bedroom wall: "She's going to die, my baby's dying, my little girl is dying." Years later I discovered she had probably overreacted, and my incarceration might not have been necessary. But there was no disclosure in families then. I wasn't even allowed to see friends, because they said my immune system was haywire. I felt like a trapped rat.

I also felt changes taking place inside my psyche. Before the illness started, I had been a mother's little sweetheart, father's little dividend. Well, I may have gone into that sickroom a sweet lamb, but I came out anything but. Perhaps it was my anger at having been imprisoned for so long. Or maybe it was the fact that the illness took place at the time when little girls begin turning into menstruating teenagers. Whatever the reason, my obedience vanished, leaving in its wake adventurousness, rebelliousness, and audacity. I became deaf to my parents' orders. Bad habits sprung up all over. Back at school, I took up with a wild crowd, smoking cigarettes and sneaking over fences. A teacher caught me, and I was suspended.

Before I could get into serious trouble at Long Beach, however, the serial mover struck again: My father announced that we were leaving home for Los Angeles. Once again my mother packed everything up, and once again we were in a new house.

Not long afterward I began to suffer different but equally severe physical symptoms. At times these pains, which attacked my lower abdomen, were crippling, but my family doctor wasn't impressed. "She's just going through menstruation," he explained, and he refused to give me an internal examination because I was a virgin. Heaven forbid he investigate and foul up my wedding night. But the pains continued until my mother finally took me to another doctor who found a cyst the size of a grapefruit on my right ovary; it was quickly removed, along with the ovary.

They insisted I could still have kids, though, which was good, because it was obvious that my mother had plans for me. As I was maturing into a young woman, she was dropping hints about marriage —nothing too obvious, just vague comments like, "It's just as easy to fall in love with a rich boy as a poor boy, honey." Another of my mother's mantras. Marry a man with money. But good marriage material was the farthest thing from my mind.

Meanwhile, my brother Gary was sent off after school to work at my father's new business, which was now a car wash—my father changed businesses as often as he moved. The idea was to teach Gary how to make money, as well as to accustom him to the work ethic. If Gary wanted something, he was going to have to earn the money to buy it.

But me? The Girl? Girls are given things. So they gave me sweaters, clothes, toys, jewelry. While my brother was taught the value of money, I was taught the value of fluttering eyelashes. Gary was being conditioned to take care of himself, and I was being conditioned to be taken care of.

My mother always said that the proper way to get what you want was through correct manipulation of The Male, although she didn't call it that. "You simply have to use good timing," she used to say, "when you want something from your father." Life was a mysterious and complicated set of negotiations to get things out of The Male.

"It's not attractive to be too smart," I was told. "It's not attractive to have a career."

This extended to schooling, where not only did I let the boys think they were brighter than I—and believe me, that wasn't always easy— there were whole subjects that I didn't even try to understand. For instance, math. I always thought I didn't have math skills, because everyone told me that girls can't add. So I sat back in math class and let all those complex numbers slide over me. My brother was good in math, though. Why? Because he was a boy. I thought boys were born multiplying numbers in their head. It's still true today. Ask a woman how she feels about math, and nine out of ten will say they're terrible at it. Once I'd have said the same, but today I sit with my chief financial officer while we do the company spreadsheets, and I can ballpark the numbers so closely he always asks why we bother with a calculator.

◆ ◆ ◆

Outside of my health, life presented few real worries, but the complications of being a girl never stopped arising. If it wasn't one thing, it was another. Like my nose. A nose is a nose, and frankly, I was fond of mine, but as I approached my late teens my mother, who spoke through hints, dropped ones like, "You know, sweetheart, your nose is lovely, but it's the wrong shape for your face."

I got the drift. "I don't want a nose job," I said.

My mother wouldn't have any of it. "You'll thank me later in life," she said. In other words, she meant that men would find me more attractive as I grew older.

My father's response was to kiss my nose and tell me it couldn't have been nicer, which was his way of saying, Don't listen to your mother. There was, however, no such thing as not listening to my mother. I got the new nose.

But the nose wasn't enough. What about weight? There were times when I must have been at least ten pounds overweight. Ten pounds! That was unthinkable! Girls had to look good, and that meant thin. Were chubby girls happy? No! How many fat girls made it to the Mickey Mouse Club?

So my mother sent me back to the doctor, with whom I was becoming close, armed with her plan for me to shed excess pounds: diet pills. And of course, I took them happily. Who doesn't swallow what your doctor gives you? It took me years to understand that my prescription was a legal introduction to speed.

I wasn't alone; half the girls in the senior class were taking them. Most of us were on something called Preludin. It sounded so harmless, like a Chopin piece for piano. Furthermore, not only did Preludin kill your appetite, it kept you wide awake while you were cramming for your exams—too, too useful.

But these pills were also teaching me a subtle lesson, one that I was learning all too well: Any time my life threatened to go awry, all I had to do was ask the doctor for a pill, and the problem would vanish. Again, I wasn't alone; we were an entire generation of women trained by our doctors in the art of judicious pill-taking.

But why worry? There I was in high school, thin, with a great nose and lots of clothes, and lots of dates. By my junior year I had gone through several boyfriends, until I met Him: Jerry, a handsome new transfer student. My heart stopped. I thought I would just die when he asked me out, and soon, like one of those pretty '50s songs, we were teenage lovers. We even came close to having real sex—but not quite. Good girls didn't do it. And I was a good girl.

After a year of college, Jerry went up to Northern California to study to become a gym teacher, while I went off to City College in Santa Monica.

My mother was thrilled. I had found marriage material! Even though Jerry wasn't rich, he was clearly the providing type, and he was getting a good education, besides.

Stay thin, look good, find a man, get married, have children. That was life. Who needed to think about education or a job? Someone else would always be there to watch over me.

Financial Independence

Don't get me wrong: Marriage can be terrific. Plenty of women get married and stay that way because they're deeply in love with a wonderful guy.

Other women stay married because they've found a reasonable compromise that suits them. For them marriage isn't about romance, but pragmatism. If it works, who's complaining?

But then there are also women who get, and stay, married because they're afraid to take responsibility for their own financial welfare.

Yet so often I've met with women who tell me that, after years of struggling to make a not-so-perfect marriage flourish, it ended anyway. In many cases, the husband then tried to keep as much of his money as possible. The wife may or may not have received a good settlement, but even so, after so many years of staying home, she often ended up without any skills to bring to the workforce. Very few women, when they divorce, receive so much money that they never have to worry, or work, again.

I wish I could shake these women and say, "If you had taken that same energy that it took to hide your feelings and live in an unhappy marriage for all those years, and gone out and found a job instead, you might have developed a great career and made a terrific living."

Which is more difficult? Living in a bad marriage, or working for a living? The working woman gets to leave her job every day and go home. The woman who stays in a marriage because she thinks it's the only way to support herself never leaves her job.

I don't mean you should leave your husband just to be financially independent. Relationships can be great. As you'll see, I've certainly been blessed with my share of wonderful men (and some who weren't so wonderful). But be with a man because you want to be with him, not because you don't think you have any other options.

Where does this instinct for letting a man take care of you come from? I can't pretend to have the answers to life's big questions, but I can interpret from my experience. And my experience tells me that environmental factors are often the answer. For instance, I have a wonderful friend named Sally who has just divorced her third husband. Intelligent, shrewd, and domineering, Sally's mother came from an excellent family, and she insisted that her daughter grow up to be the most perfect specimen yet—no blots, blotches, blemishes. Sally's earliest memories are of her mother dressing her in pretty gowns and parading her in front of all the boys. She hired private tutors to teach

Sally manners and dance professionals to teach her movement, as well as encouraging her to spend hours brushing her hair and making up her face.

Sally indeed grew up to be beautiful, smart, and an excellent dancer. Hungry for achievement, Sally's mother pushed her into both acting and modeling. She shoved and cajoled, and Sally responded, winning modeling jobs and occasional parts in local theater productions.

Sally's mother never encouraged her to use her mind, which was as sharp as her looks, because this kind of training really has just one goal: to land a man. And for that, Sally's mother thought, you only need the right appearance. Other women don't do things for you because you look good. But many men do.

Sally's first marriage to a wealthy businessman lasted only a few years and left her with little money, due to her husband's shrewd lawyers. Sally's next husband was even wealthier, but that marriage didn't last long, either, and Sally went through the more generous settlement quickly, telling herself that she needed to spend the money to soothe the pain.

Sally was now approaching an age where the lack of financial security was risky. But instead of launching a career, she set her sights on Jay, one of the richest men in her home state. Jay, twice as old as Sally, was delighted by her attentions, but, nobody's fool, he demanded that Sally sign a rigorous prenuptial agreement, one which Sally failed to examine closely.

She didn't examine Jay well enough either. Although she knew he wasn't a bargain, she wasn't prepared for his abusive behavior. Jay treated Sally alternately like an employee, a child, and a pet, telling her what to wear, how to eat, when to speak. It wasn't long before he was cheating on her, too.

Sally gritted her teeth and bore it all, but then, just short of their tenth anniversary, Jay announced that he wanted a divorce. All Sally had now was the prenuptial agreement, but still she had to hire a lawyer, and eventually she received, along with her settlement, huge legal bills. Now she's on her own, without the money to live as she'd grown accustomed.

Sally gave herself to marriage in return for security as well as all the material possessions she could want. Now she has neither the security nor the possessions. I told her that if she had only gone out and found a job after that first marriage, by this time she'd be much wealthier and probably happier.

Whenever I tell Sally's story to other women, they're sympathetic, but I notice that those in situations similar to Sally's don't believe such bad luck will happen to them. And maybe, if they're fortunate, it won't. But what if it does? Do they have the knowledge and financial security to survive?

That's just one story. The tragedy is that I run into so many others. And it's certainly not always the mother's fault. Sometimes the fault belongs with the father; sometimes, an entire family; and many times there's no obvious reason—or, perhaps, the reasons are so endemic to our society that their roots defy exploration. Nonetheless, women still lag behind men in terms of financial knowledge, and they often choose a mate to avoid that responsibility, as in the case of Sally, who was smart, but who married for money rather than love.

Still, I often think, why shouldn't women be lagging? After all, we started so much later. Since the beginning of history men have been physically stronger. They controlled the food. They controlled the women. Did you ever read that book about Neanderthal life, *The Clan of the Cave Bear*? The strong man goes out and hunts for the food, and then comes home and says to the woman, "Okay, woman, here's the food. Assume the position." I still see this attitude today, in the type of man who still says, "Okay, woman, here's the money. Assume the position."

I've even run into men who forbid women from any involvement whatsoever with the family money. The other night at a party, I was introduced to a couple; the man told me that he'd heard about my seminars from our hostess and had prohibited his wife from attending them. I assumed he was joking. He wasn't. "I take care of the finances," he said, turning adamant and angry.

"I'm not pitting men against women," I said.

The man scowled, while his wife smiled nervously and swore that she didn't want to hear anything I had to offer. I tried to explain to this man that I'm not trying to force married women to take control of the family finances. I just want the wife to know where she stands if her husband gets hit by a truck. Is a woman asking for too much if she asks for knowledge?

Chapter 3

Marriage, and Budgeting

There is a gigantic difference between earning a great deal of
money and being rich.
Marlene Dietrich

*S*ometimes it seems that no matter how much you plan for life,
life has plans of its own. When Jerry decided to go away to school, he
unwittingly doomed our relationship. I was too insecure to deal with
this kind of separation. I'd already developed that urgent need for the
right hairstyle, the right clothes, the right figure. I also needed the
right assurance that all these things were indeed perfect. And since
Jerry wasn't around to compliment me, I looked for someone else to
do it.

When the fall began, I was going to a school near the beach, but it
wasn't long before I was going to the beach near the school. It didn't
take schooling to discover how many cute male friends you could
make by wearing an itsy-bitsy bikini. I wasn't ready for marriage yet. I
was only ready for fun.

My mother was furious I'd broken off the engagement.

Then I decided to get my own apartment.

Both my parents became furious. "You're not moving out," my
father said. "You're not quitting school," my mother said. "You're not
getting your own apartment," my father said. "You're not living at the
beach," my mother said.

"And above all," they both said, "you're not getting a job!"

A job? What an insane notion!

My father put his foot down, and there was no getting around it, he had quite a foot. Although loving and kind, he was the original control freak, and he did it by keeping us dependent on him. He was a decent man, and I'm sure he thought all this was for our own good, but in his world, a woman shouldn't depend on herself. That's what men were for.

Dropping out of school was easy, however; not even Lou could force me to attend classes. He tried cutting me off, but my mother was too nice not to sneak me whatever money I needed.

My days and nights were now filled with clubs, beaches, and dancing, until one night I met a slick salesman named Bob, the kind of guy who'd been there, done that, before anyone else had even thought about it. An older man (in his late twenties) Bob taught me what every woman should know about life, and night life, too—although, despite his best efforts, I steadfastly remained a virgin. Bob also introduced me to marijuana, which was fairly rare at this time.

But I yearned for more independence, so one day, while my parents were safely vacationing in Hawaii, I rented myself an apartment and found a job as a receptionist for a business that represented itself as a correspondence school for supermarket checkers. My parents were angry but they surrendered for the time being. In the next few months, I saw some pretty unusual characters at work. My boss was always having me cash checks at the bank for different men, all of whom seemed to come from south Florida. Then my father discovered that the business was owned by gangster Mickey Cohen, and insisted I quit.

I refused, of course. Soon I moved to a new apartment north of Sunset Boulevard, where the scene was crazy kids and raucous rock 'n' roll. On the brink, my father sent over a man to bring me home physically. Although I was small, I was stubborn, and a bout of kicking and screaming convinced the man to leave me alone. Eventually my folks agreed that I could live in my own place as long as it wasn't in that neighborhood. And the job ended when Mickey Cohen went to prison.

That was in 1962. I was turning 21, and my mother was worried sick about the direction of my life, as well as the men in it: Where were the engagement rings, the future in-laws? I listened to her, a little, and moved into a new place, where I finally met Prince Charming: Martin. Twenty-two-year-old, funny, married-but-getting-an-annulment, tall, dark-haired Martin, who wore a three-piece suit to work. The key word here was "work." The other men I'd been seeing were party animals. Here was a man as cute as the others but who held a regular job. Didn't my mother say she wanted me to date someone responsible?

Within a few weeks, Martin decided we were meant for each other. The moment they heard about this, my parents packed me off to Brooklyn and my aunt Sylvia. Even though he wore a suit and had a job and even was Jewish, my parents couldn't abide Martin.

Sylvia and Uncle Sol, a milkman, kept a kosher home. "Don't touch that fork!" someone was always telling me. But since I didn't know anything about kosher, I used the wrong silverware every time. The improper use of a utensil requires its burial, so it wasn't long before Sylvia and Sol had a cemetery of forks.

Neither Sylvia nor Sol had the time to watch me all day, so I soon escaped to Manhattan, where I met a man so sexy that, tired of virginity, I ended that stage of my life. What a relief.

My parents, whose eyes, apparently, were everywhere, soon discovered I was dating. "He's half-Jewish," I lied, but the ruse didn't work, and they pulled me back to California. They probably figured, if I was going to misbehave, I might as well do it at home.

Living in California and being with Martin again felt like being a deer in the sights of some relentless hunter's rifle. "Marry me" was all Martin could say. It was like dating a lonely parrot. "Marry me, marry me, marry me."

Perhaps I never would have if he hadn't hounded me so, but I liked the flattery and the attention, and, deeply concerned about my general lack of purpose, I gave his proposal careful consideration. My life was overly chaotic and a calming influence might help. So I consented, although my gut warned me not to do it. Every time I don't follow my instincts, I've made a mistake.

After my parents met Martin's parents, they tried to stop the marriage by bribing me with a trip to Europe and a new car. But instead, that cinched it. I'd never gotten over that rebellious streak, so now I'd show them. After all, I was delivering a husband who had a job and a suit. Did they have to like him, too?

My parents surrendered, but they could never tolerate Martin, with his flashy clothes, showy jewelry, and arrogant ways. He was the kind of guy who made noise wherever he went, the type who walks into a restaurant and snaps his fingers, demanding attention. My mother thought a good man was a quiet man. Martin was about as quiet as a yard crew. It was like marrying a leaf blower.

By this time my father had switched businesses once more and was building bowling alleys. Making a good deal of money, Dad still insisted on living in an apartment. Whenever we asked about moving into a house, he always responded that taxes were killing him and that real estate was a lousy investment. We didn't question him.

For Martin's and my wedding, he offered us either a big ceremony (which would be throwing the money away, he added), or $5,000 with which we could furnish a house. We took curtain number two: the money. So the wedding took place at my parents' apartment and off we went to Las Vegas for our honeymoon. There Martin gambled, we had our wedding night, and then we came home.

So this was marriage.

Martin's father, an auctioneer, hired his son at a good wage. Me? I stayed home, although I wanted a job. But Martin said, "No. I take care of you." And since I believed then that when a man talks, a woman listens, I learned to dust the house, make the beds, and cook. Martin's every wish was my command. I was his personal genie in a bottle.

He also told my parents I still smoked marijuana. What kind of husband rats on you?

It was a bad sign.

Other Women's Stories

Throughout this book, I'll be talking about some of the circumstances and finances of various women I've met over the last few years. But before I do, let me make it clear that investment guidance is personal and specific, and I need a great deal of information about any individual before I can help her. The recommendations I've made here aren't intended for you, personally. They're included to give you a rough idea of other women's needs, and how we at The Resnick Group have tried to meet them.

What this book will not do is promise that with our help, you can beat the experts and make millions. If books that make such claims really worked, wouldn't millions of people have already bought them and made however many millions of dollars? And wouldn't their friends have noticed how successful they were, and also have bought the book, and made millions too? And their friends, and their friends, and so on? Wouldn't we all be rich by now?

Well, we're not all rich. No one's ever published a book that truly guaranteed financial success.

In fact, not all of the women whose lives we'll explore are even participating in our money-management program. Some of them didn't choose to, and some couldn't afford it. But as the range of ages and income here suggests, we do try to work with as many different types of women as possible. And while a majority of our clients are wealthy, we also work with women who aren't rich to help get them started, through seminars and one-on-one meetings. And if a close friend asks me to talk to a friend in trouble, I don't refuse. You meet the same people going up as going down.

A few more caveats: Please remember that, when we talk about a 10 percent average return in someone's portfolio, this means an average of the returns in bad years plus the returns in good years, as well as an average of various performances in the portfolio itself. For every item in a real portfolio to return 10 percent each year is a statistical improbability.

Moreover, the portfolios discussed in these pages are highly abbreviated summaries, snapshots of the real thing. I'm using them to illustrate real-life issues and possible answers. They aren't in any way portfolios you should duplicate.

Finally, neither I nor anyone else at my firm would ever consider breaking a client's confidence, any more than a good doctor or analyst would. Therefore, I have disguised these women's identities to make them unrecognizable.

Jennifer

Now, let me tell you about Jennifer, who's a 28-year-old agent at a theatrical talent group earning $35,000 a year. She's been with her company since she graduated from college seven years ago; the agency gives her a good benefits package, including health insurance and a 401(k).

Jennifer had saved $35,000—some of it came from her salary, some was a gift from her parents, and some came from her grandmother's estate. "That's a great deal of money to have saved at your age," I told her, even if part of it came to her through an inheritance. Many people prefer to spend windfalls rather than put them in the bank. I was impressed.

Jennifer is very independent-minded, willing to take risks, and she wants to participate herself in any investment activities that I'd support, but she works so hard that she has little time left in her day for anything except dating, exercise, and sleep. Her goal is to build a nest egg, because someday she'd like to start her own agency.

The first thing we did was to study her expenses, insurance, and budgets. One thing we discovered was a serious anomaly in her health package, which did not have disability insurance (see page 113). This is a must, I told her—an absolute must. At her age Jennifer is much more likely to get sick than to die. As they say, if you die, you won't need food, clothes, or shelter, but if you become ill, you'll still be hungry and you'll still need a place to live.

"Who's going to take care of you in case you come down with something serious? Do you have family that would help you?" I asked, but Jennifer just shrugged, for like most people her age, she hadn't given it any thought.

"Not really," she said. Her parents were retired and on a fixed income, while her older sister was married and doing well, but with two kids she had no discretionary savings. "Do I really need to buy that kind of insurance now?" she asked.

Not only was the answer yes, I told her, but disability insurance is much cheaper to purchase at 28 than later in life. When I first bought it I was over 40, and so it cost me an arm and a leg, but I've had it ever since.

We then discussed Jennifer's savings, which looked quite healthy for someone her age. But I discovered that Jennifer hadn't told me that she also had debt—she owed just a little over $10,000 on her credit cards.

"So you really only have $25,000 saved," I said.

Jennifer wanted to dispute this, but the logic is unassailable. The interest on her $10,000 credit card debt is 17 percent a year. From December 1960 to December 1995, the Standard & Poor's average has increased 10.7 percent—in other words, it's tough for excellent investors to make 17 percent year after year. (The Standard & Poor's index includes 500 stocks and is considered the benchmark for large-stock investors.) So even if I could invest Jennifer's $10,000 and make a solid 10 percent, she'd still be losing money on it.

So, by paying that $10,000 off right now, Jennifer immediately starts to save money.

Then we looked over her expenses. Last year, after taxes, Jennifer netted about $28,000. Her yearly rent was $7,800 (she shares an apartment with a friend), and between food, clothes, and her car, she was spending another $16,800. This left her $3,400 a year to save, which is excellent—it's about 10 percent of her gross earnings. If she can get into that saving habit, when she's making $150,000 a year, she'll be saving $15,000 annually.

She wasn't sure she could do that this year, though, because she wanted a new wardrobe. "Nope," I said. "Leave that savings in your budget. You have to learn to prioritize. Savings comes first, so buy a few nice pieces, but don't go overboard. Because if you continue to save as you've been doing, between that and the compounding effect on your investments, you're on your way to building a nice bundle for yourself."

We talked more about what Jennifer wanted from her life. At this point her priority is to save enough money to start her own business.

"Why?" I asked. It turned out that Jennifer liked being an agent, but her company wasn't known for moving people through the ranks, and she didn't see any significant financial benefits from staying put long

term. *This job was a good stepping-stone, but not necessarily perma-*
nent, so Jennifer was wise to be saving carefully now, just in case.

I suggested this plan for her (for more information and definitions on
the specifics mentioned, see the section on investing, page 119): mutual
funds that leaned more toward stocks, since Jennifer, being young,
doesn't need the income of a bond portfolio. For the short term, she
needs a reserve fund. For the long term, what she can use most is
growth. And because she's so young, she can also weather a few bad
years in the market, since her investment horizons are long-term rather
than short-term. If she's patient, time will be on her side and she can
enjoy the magic of compounding and seeing her money grow.

I told Jennifer to pay off her $10,000 credit card debt first, and then
put aside money for an emergency fund. (I suggested that she put
$6,000 into a money market fund, where she might be less tempted to
touch it than if it were at a bank, and another $6,000 into intermedi-
ate term bonds, which are not quite as safe as cash, but have a higher
yield and are very conservative.) The balance was put into a diverse
group of funds made up of large cap stocks, small cap stocks, a foreign
diversified stock fund, and a small amount of the sum in an income
fund specializing in intermediate U.S. bonds (this means bonds that
mature in about ten years, as opposed to short two-year bonds, or
long thirty-year bonds). This way, she can begin creating a diversified
portfolio.

Finally, I told her that I admired her desire to start her own business,
but in the meantime she should be sure that her current job pays her
what she's worth. "Go in there and tell them how good you are!" I said.

◆ ◆ ◆

*A*ctually, Martin's tattletale tendencies were much more than a bad
sign. Our marriage turned out to be, in a word, appalling. When I'd
ask for new clothes, he'd tell me to forget about it, although he did let
me have one nice outfit for our evenings out, so that I wouldn't make
him look bad. He made the money, he spent the money, and my role
was to take care of him. I felt like his personal slave. Where was Abe
Lincoln when you needed him?

For instance, after work Martin used to run his finger along a book-shelf, and if he found dust, he wasn't shy about letting me know. "What the hell were you doing today?" he'd ask. "Eating bonbons?" He examined the rim of the toilet bowl. "This is filthy—get back here and scrub!" This went on for months without a word of protest on my part.

One day, he found that I had folded the bathroom towels into halves, rather than into thirds, like any intelligent maid. "You screwed up again," he said.

"Who the hell do you think you are?" I snapped. I was holding a can of cleanser in my hand at the moment, since I'd been scrubbing the toilet for the tenth time that day, and I threw it at his head. Unfortunately (for me), I had bad aim.

Martin responded by doing what any sensible, red-blooded Ameri-can male would do. He hauled off and swung at a door, putting his fist through it. So manly. He certainly seemed impressed with himself, cursing like a hero.

This wasn't my idea of a marriage. Slowly, but quite surely, I started gaining weight, going from a size five to a size ten in a matter of months. My self-esteem withered from the scent of bleaches and cleansers and ammonia. I felt like the little girl in a fairy tale who gets imprisoned by the wicked witch, except that I'd married the witch, his name was Martin, and he grew worse and worse.

After one year, I wanted out. I called my mother and confessed that her worst fears were true.

"I'll help you pack," she said. She even brought my grandmother along, to get me out faster. But the timing was bad. Before my mother could even open the suitcase, the phone rang. Martin's doctor was on the line, with the results of Martin's recent physical.

"He's sick," the doctor said.

"Leave him anyway," my grandmother snapped—she was old, maybe, but no fool. My mother burst into tears, however, because she knew I'd stay. "How can I leave a sick man?" I asked.

Martin, upon hearing about the doctor's phone call, wept like a baby. The doctor insisted I nurse him, so suddenly I was the Florence

Nightingale of the Southland, giving Martin injections, feeding him, nursing him.

For the moment, he was nice to me.

I got pregnant, which was what Martin most wanted. Now he really seemed to turn a corner—caring for me, pampering me; no good clothes, but still, he was pleasant.

In all this time I'd learned nothing about money. I felt I was entitled only to what Martin was willing to dole out. It never entered my mind to create a budget. I couldn't have done it if you'd put a gun to my head. I might have taken that gun and shot Martin with it, but that wouldn't have solved my financial problems. It just would have made me happier.

Budgeting

Recently one of my associates asked me to meet with an old high school friend of hers. Ellen, a 29-year-old lawyer, was married to Mike, a 28-year-old lawyer. Between them, they're making over $100,000 a year, excellent at such a young age. They love the fact that they already earn more than either of their parents ever did—it makes them feel rich, and they foresee a life where money won't be their worst issue.

But as Ellen reluctantly admitted when we met, not everything was easy. Besides paying back student loans, Ellen was four months pregnant, and the couple was looking to buy a house. And, their car had been dented in an accident and wasn't fully covered by insurance. Finally, because Mike's mother was broke, he was sending her money on a regular basis.

When I asked Ellen how these additional expenses affected her budget, she looked surprised. "Budget?" she asked, as though I had shifted the conversation into Swahili. Her eyebrows practically darted off her forehead. "We don't need to budget," she said. "Look how much we make."

Well, it didn't take long to bring that balloon down to earth. As much as Ellen and Mike were making each month, they were already spending more than they brought home. Here was a catastrophe begging to happen.

I'm continually startled by how few women who need to put together a budget actually do so. Not that every woman must—certainly some earn enough that they don't have to worry, and others are so instinctively budget-minded they don't need one. But for those who do need a budget—and that's the majority of women we meet—we hand them two things: a **cash flow statement,** and a **balance sheet.**

BALANCE SHEET—ASSETS

Cash/Cash Equivalents

Checking Account   _____

Savings Account   _____

Money Market Account   _____

Life Insurance Cash Value   _____

Total Cash Assets: _____

Invested Assets

Stocks   _____

Bonds   _____

Limited Partnerships   _____

IRAs/Qualified Pensions   _____

Annuities   _____

Real Estate   _____

Closely Held Corporations   _____

Total Invested Assets: _____

Use Assets

Residence(s)   _____

Automobiles   _____

Personal Property   _____

Total Use Assets: _____

BALANCE SHEET—LIABILITIES

Credit Card Balances   _____
Auto Loan Balances   _____
Mortgage Loan Balances   _____
Other   _____

Total Liabilities: _____

BALANCE SHEET—NET WORTH

Total Assets: _____
(minus)   _____
Total Liabilities: _____

NET WORTH: _____

CASH FLOW STATEMENT—EXPENSES

Fixed Monthly Expenses
Savings and Investments   _____
Mortgage or Rent   _____
Real Estate Taxes   _____
Automobile Loans   _____
Personal Loans   _____
Income Taxes   _____
Insurance Premiums: Home, Auto, Medical,
  Disability, Life   _____
Utilities: Gas, Electric, Water   _____
Food   _____
Education   _____
Child Care   _____
Other   _____

Total Fixed Expenses: _____

Variable Monthly Expenses

Charge Accounts _____

Transportation _____

Household Maintenance and Repair _____

Furnishings _____

Telephone _____

Clothing _____

Club Dues _____

Entertainment _____

Vacations _____

Other _____

Total Variable Expenses: _____

Total Monthly Expenses: _____

INCOME STATEMENT—INCOME

Monthly Income _____

Wages, Salary, Tips _____

Dividends from Stocks, Mutual Funds, etc. _____

Interest on Savings Accounts, CDs, Bonds, etc. _____

Capital Gains _____

Other Pensions, Royalties, etc. _____

Total Monthly Income: _____

INCOME STATEMENT—NET CASH FLOW

Total Monthly Income: _____

(minus)

Total Expenses: _____

NET CASH FLOW: _____

First, cash flow: List your fixed monthly expenses, such as your rent or mortgage payment, automobile loans, food, etc. Then list your variable monthly expenses, such as clothing and vacations, and add the two figures. Next, determine your income by adding your after-tax monthly wages, interest, and so on. Finally, subtract your expenses from your income to see how much you have left. This should be a positive number—otherwise, you'll need some immediate help. If you're in the black, now you can figure out how much you can afford to save, and how much you can afford to spend.

A balance sheet is equally easy. Write down your assets on the appropriate line: money in the bank, the value of your home, and "use" assets (the money you have invested in your house or condo, your car, or other items you use). Next, list your liabilities: your debts to the bank for your car, home, credit cards, etc. Then subtract your liabilities from your assets, and voilà! That's how much you're worth. Once again, I hope it's a positive number. Negatives are exactly that—negative.

Budgeting is a simple matter. All it signifies is the ability to live within your means. Once you've completed the cash flow and balance forms, you can decide if you're spending too much and if so, where to cut back. Did you really need that new suit, or that new puppy, or that new nose? The car repair isn't discretionary; you can't get to work without the car. But you *can* do without the manicure every week. In fact, maybe you can't afford the manicure at all. Maybe that manicure is really your savings account. Maybe that trip to Europe is really your IRA.

A line-by-line look at your budget gives you a picture of your finances, and, like any picture, it speaks for itself, talking back to you, giving you all the information you need. Sometimes, it'll slap you right in the face.

For instance, I have one client, Angela, who told me on our first meeting that she spent $10,000 a month. Considering how much money she was worth, I said, "Great. You can save five thousand dollars a month, too."

However, once we prepared her cash flow statement, it turned out that Angela was actually spending $24,000 a month! Yet she refused to believe me. "I'd know if I were spending that much," she insisted.

In this case, we'd prepared the statement from Angela's actual bills over the past six months. So how could she deny it? But she did. It reminded me of the husband's line when his wife catches him in bed with another woman: "Who are you going to believe, me or your eyes?" he asks.

The time you most need a budget is when you're deluding yourself. It helps to see it in writing, or you'll keep bleeding. It's very simple. If you take out more stones than you put in, eventually the bucket will be empty. Angela was living off her income and also withdrawing her principal to keep up her spending; if she had continued this way, she would have gone through all her money within a few years. Like many of us, she had an excuse for every month she spent too much. And it was almost always a nonrecurring expense, like the new television, or the week at a spa. Sound familiar?

As I said, not every woman needs a budget. Some people naturally save money. The poorest aunt in my family ended up saving more money than my mother. Mom used to laugh at her and all her envelopes: one for the savings account, one for the phone, one for the electricity, but my aunt ended up secure—not rich, but comfortable. She was a realist, and a good thing too; now she's 81. If you're a realist, then perhaps you don't need a budget. But if you're not—and there's no shame in it—then sit down and do one. Get real! Today!

Chapter 4

Divorce, and Desperation

And the trouble is, if you don't risk anything, you risk even more.

Erica Jong

*B*ack in 1965, when a woman had a baby, she shared a hospital room, and my roommate turned out to be an old high school friend whose parents had invented a doll and named it after her. So there I was, sharing labor with the eponymous Barbie, and the experience was actually as effortless as it sounds, since Audrey couldn't have been easier to deliver, and now there she was, my love, my child, my salvation. Perhaps life wasn't so bad.

Then again, perhaps it was. The night I came home from the hospital, Martin, recovered from his sickness, greeted me with those supportive words every new mother wants to hear: "I'm having people for dinner. Whatcha gonna make?"

No one in my family had ever been divorced, but I was willing to forge new territory. My fantasy life swelled like a pregnant belly. I started dreaming about Martin's death. How many ways did I kill him? Let me count. I pictured him dying of poison, choking on food, falling out a window—but my all-time personal favorite, because he used to take so many business trips, was driving off a cliff. Even with a dark veil, I used to wonder, could I hide my happiness at his funeral?

We were constantly fighting. He'd yell, I'd cry. I'd yell, he'd cry. He'd shout, I'd run away. It wasn't much fun.

Before Audrey was a year old, the doctor decided she needed surgery for a malfunctioning urethra. I wasn't feeling too well, either, so when I went to the doctor with Audrey for the surgery, I asked him to examine me, too.

"You're pregnant," he said.

Martin didn't show up at the hospital for Audrey's operation. "Take care of it yourself," he said.

Meanwhile, I was considering an abortion, because I knew this marriage wouldn't last much longer. It was bad enough to survive as a divorcée with one child, I thought, but to have two might make the odds insurmountable. Still, I also doubted I'd ever marry again, and I wanted Audrey to have a younger sibling.

I sat Martin down and told him that I was considering an abortion. What could I have been thinking? Martin immediately saw a way to curry favor with my parents, and so he ran to my mother, sobbing all the way about how much he wanted that child, and for a moment—a brief one—he was a hero. Fran was furious. An abortion was beyond the pale.

Meanwhile, my gynecologist recommended that I see a psychiatrist. So I did, all the while weeping about my unhappy life with Martin. The psychiatrist asked to see him a few times, too, and afterward said, "I've never told this to anyone before, but you must listen to me and leave this man. He will destroy you. Even if he had therapy five days a week for five years, I wouldn't guarantee he'd change.

"And once you've done that," he continued, "continue your own therapy and discover what got you into this marriage to begin with, and what has kept you there for four years."

A few days later, Martin announced, "I bought us a house in the valley."

My own family had prepared me for this kind of an announcement, but the difference was, when my father made his frequent moves, the rest of our family *wanted* to move with him.

"I'm leaving you," I said.

"You didn't hear me," said Martin. "I bought a house. We're moving."

"I'm leaving you," I said.

"I bought a house," he said.

This brilliant exchange could have lasted forever, but I didn't want to spend eternity arguing with Martin, so I gave in for the moment. We moved, but I didn't hang my paintings in my new house, and for me, no paintings means it's a no-go.

"I'm leaving you," I said, once he had moved himself in.

"What are you going to do?" he said. "You've got a kid and another in the oven and you're fat and ugly."

This conversation wasn't going anywhere, so I did. I ran into my room, slammed the door, and cried. "Who's going to support you?" he called after me. "Who do you think you're kidding?"

Whenever life lets me down, my body tends to speak up. During my next examination my doctor found a tumor on my back and recommended it be removed immediately. The tumor was benign, but it laid me up for a few weeks. First, I had the baby, then I had the operation—all alone. But now there was Stacey, who turned out to be the loving sister I'd wanted for Audrey. The girls, the best things in my life, were well worth the marriage.

A few weeks later, at a party, I heard Martin tell a friend, "She's talking about leaving. Her father's in the Mafia, so I have to worry, because they could come after me."

I was furious—inventing lies about my family; I'd had it. I took a wineglass, broke it, and went after him. But I dropped the glass, became embarrassed, and then ran outside and down a hill. There I fell, hurting myself badly, and lay in the street, bleeding from scratches up and down my legs. Today the lingering scars remind me never to take such abuse again.

Martin strolled over to where I'd fallen and, without offering to help, asked, "Why are you doing this to yourself?"

It was a damned good question—why was I doing this? A few days later, after Martin left town on a business trip, I took action, changing all the locks on the house. When he returned, I wouldn't let him inside. "You don't live here anymore," I said.

He drove off angrily, but he called a few hours later to ask for his clock radio. His clock radio? That was all he wanted? "Come and get it," I said sweetly.

When he drove back, I met him in the driveway. "Here's your clock radio," I said, and smashed it to pieces on the ground.

I called Dad. "I have some good news and some bad news," I told him. "My head is finally together, and I want a divorce."

"What's the bad news?" he asked. An hour later he was helping me pack up the children's things, along with a few personal items of mine, and we all took off. We dumped the wedding album in the garbage.

Now the real wars started. Martin contested the divorce, and the court forced me to see a reconciliation counselor. No-fault divorce didn't exist yet. Still, the counseling lasted only one visit. "I'm not staying with him," I said, and that ended it.

"Her father's rich," Martin told the judge. "Let him support her."

My father, furious, wanted me to fight, but eventually we gave up, and Dad assumed sole responsibility for taking care of my children.

Many years later, after three more wives, Martin went to prison for customs fraud. Sometimes, late at night, lying awake thinking about my life, I remember that, and it makes me smile.

Marcy

Thirty-three years old—somewhat older than I was at the time I was divorced—Marcy is divorcing her one and only husband, Ted, to whom she's been married for more than ten years. Marcy was a high school teacher when she met Ted, an accountant many years older than she, and she left her job to raise their two kids, who are now seven and nine years old. The couple has joint custody.

From the divorce Marcy has been awarded a lump sum settlement of $250,000, along with the house and child support of $900 a month. The divorce wasn't pleasant—Ted's marrying his secretary—but he isn't a deadbeat dad, either, as far as Marcy can tell at this point.

Marcy has returned to teaching, at a salary of $32,000 a year. Since the child support isn't taxable, this leaves her with a net income of somewhat more than $3,000 a month (after taxes).

Marcy hadn't thought much about her financial future: She always assumed she'd live with Ted and he'd take care of her. Marcy's needs aren't great: She wants to continue her basic life-style, and she'd like to guarantee that her kids can attend college, because even though Ted promises to help, Marcy doesn't trust him anymore.

Marcy's parents have a little money, but she can't count on an inheritance, because they're both relatively young and healthy and could live for several more decades, or could go through their money in nursing-home costs.

Marcy is timid, and scared to be on her own. She came to me because she didn't know what to do with her $250,000, as well as the rest of her finances.

First we went over her monthly expenses: her overhead, i.e., the money she spends on the house and kids, clothes, food, and so on. We discovered that her expenses almost exactly equaled her income, so she can't put any money away for the time being. In some ways Marcy has been quite lucky: Her parents have helped with the house's mortgage, so she doesn't need to move, and her kids are going to the school where she teaches, so day care isn't an issue either.

Since her ultimate goal is to send the kids to college, Marcy wondered if the entire $250,000 should be allotted to that. But I reminded her that if she spent all the money on education, she'd be making herself vulnerable.

"Can I put the kids through college without touching it?" she asked.

The answer was, "I think so." First, Marcy needs to set aside about $20,000 and keep it liquid, which could entail, for instance, putting it in a money market account in case of family emergencies. The other $230,000 needs to be grown.

At this point we talked about risk, as I do with almost all the women I see. The notion that there was no absolute guarantee she couldn't lose all her money worried Marcy, for she had nothing else to count on. Her teacher's pension was adequate, but it wouldn't pay her enough to continue her current life-style.

"How nervous are you?" I asked.

"Quite," she said. "I can teach for a long time, but I'll never make much money."

We then discussed the unlikelihood of Marcy's money dwindling to zero, and why careful, prudent investing was not as risky as she thought. We also discussed what would happen if Marcy didn't invest the money, but put it in the bank for ten years: how the low interest rate at a bank, combined with taxes and inflation, would leave her about where she is now.

The fact is, if Marcy puts the money aside, and doesn't touch it for ten years, investments at 10 percent should bring her $230,000 up to about $597,000 before any taxes, or enough money to pay for her children's college education and keep enough principal for her to grow for her retirement.

Now, if Marcy averages a more aggressive 14 percent over these ten years, she'll have about $853,000 before taxes, although it will be a much more risky course. And, on the other hand, if Marcy wants to invest her money at a very conservative 6 percent average interest rate, over ten years she'll have about $412,000.

In other words, for Marcy's $230,000 to become worth as much as she needs, she must have growth in her portfolio, and to do that, she needs to get into equity.

My particular advice concerning her portfolio was to put 65 percent of her money into equities (stocks) and 35 percent into fixed-income funds (bonds)—the 65 percent allocated into individual large cap stocks and small caps, with a small percentage put into a diversified international stock fund (again, for more information on these stocks and bonds, see the chapter on investing, page 117).

On the fixed income side, I recommended Marcy diversify by including intermediate government bonds, some corporate bonds including a small allocation to high-yield bonds, and medium-term Treasuries.

I used some high-yield bonds as well, because, although they can be risky, it's a market I trust and understand.

Marcy's particular allocation is heavily weighted toward growth because she's young, and can grow her assets over many years. Like Jennifer, she can withstand a down cycle in the stock market because, historically, every down cycle has been preceded by a much larger up cycle.

Marcy also wanted to know if she could afford to send her kids to a top-rated private school which, given the way colleges have been raising their tuition, could cost something like $80 million by that time.

"Get a grip, please," I said. Marcy can offer her children a perfectly good education without sacrificing her own security. The point here is balance. "If you can't afford Stanford, be a realist," I said. "Look at the options you can afford. Without some other financial assistance, you can only do what you can do.

"You have to take care of your own life," I continued. "You don't want to be a victim of the system when you grow old. You want choices. Don't spend your last nickel on your kids, or on anything else, for that matter."

We also discussed Marcy's other needs, such as making sure that she had adequate life insurance for the children. Her current policy is for $100,000, sponsored through her workplace. That's a good amount, I said, but I thought she should consider more, through term insurance, because Marcy needs the policy only while the kids are young, and since she wants to put her money into other investments for the time being, I didn't feel she required more expensive whole-life insurance. (If this sounds as confusing to you as it once did to me, see the section on insurance, page 105.)

Finally, I recommended that Marcy consult an estate planner, because now more on her own than ever, she needs a will and a living trust.

◆ ◆ ◆

*N*ow I was a divorcée, the first in my family, and the pressure was on. Not from society—from my mother.

"You have two children. You should think about marriage."

She was sitting at my kitchen table, holding my wrists, looking straight into my face—sad blue eyes meeting sad brown ones. "I'll be happy when I see you settled," she said. "I'll be happy when you find a husband," she meant.

"The kids are young and still appealing," she said. "The kids won't be okay until you find a husband," she meant.

She wasn't trying to hurt me. This was her attempt to help, and that meant finding me a man. It never occurred to her to say, "Now's the time to figure out how to make a living."

I'm sure my mother was taking some heat from her friends about me, but I was only a few years ahead of the curve. Soon everyone else was getting a divorce, and she could console her friends about their daughters, too.

My father was more supportive. "Don't listen to your mother," he said. "You don't have to marry. I'll support you."

This sounded nice at the time, but still no one was saying, "Why don't you go and try to develop a skill, and take care of the kids without anyone else's help?"

It quickly seemed that everyone in the world had something to say about my situation, and it was startling how similar everyone sounded: Find a man, get married, settle down. Then, four months after my divorce, my body spoke out too, but unfortunately it chose its usual crisis-related fashion to do so. I went in to the doctor for a routine checkup, and went home with a diagnosis of cervical cancer. I was 26, overweight, depressed, alone, and now I had a deadly disease.

Patti, my new next-door neighbor, saw how upset I was, and because she wanted to help, offered me a little red pill.

"What is it?" I asked.

"Seconal," she said.

"Why would I want to take a sleeping pill during the daytime?" I asked.

"Trust me," Patti said.

So I did. And sure enough, soon I was feeling great.

My Preludin had acclimated me to the notion that pills could solve any problem. Seconals confirmed it. When I exhausted Patti's supply, I sought out a doctor who conscientiously gave me a prescription. Why? "Can't sleep," I said, which was reason enough in those days. Back then, pills came unaccompanied by a sense of wrongdoing. This was the decade where everyone knew that the answer to life's problems was mother's little helper. All across America doctors were prescribing millions of pills to women each year. Today, if you look up Seconal in a medical guide, you'll learn that it can cause physical addiction, along with such side effects as confusion, nausea, skin rash, vomiting, and, if taken in large enough amounts, death. Then, all you knew was that it promised a pleasant night's sleep, or a pleasant day avoiding reality.

My doctor told me to take them "whenever necessary." I did. And I was still on Preludin, too, to lose weight, so essentially these good doctors were making sure that I had easy access to uppers and downers. Was this a drug problem? I didn't think so, and anyway, I was hardly getting them off the street. I consoled myself with the thought that I needed them to avoid feeling helpless, so convinced was I that a withering death from cancer lay around the corner.

The surgery, however, was successful. Still, I kept the pills, because the doctors kept prescribing them. Who argues with doctors, particularly when they've proved themselves capable of removing death from your body?

Cancer was easier to eradicate than Martin, who had now decided that he wanted me back. Somehow I didn't trust this abrupt love. Was his house dirty? His oven encrusted? Perhaps he'd found a smudge on his toilet.

I refused a reconciliation. He retaliated. The judge had given him visiting rights to the children, and so Martin started showing up every Sunday with Susan, his girlfriend and soon-to-be wife number three. Susan was pretty, with dark hair tied up in back with a big, bright ribbon. The first time I saw it I thought, Good—someday she'll need it to strangle him.

But eventually Martin stopped seeing the kids, and he disappeared from my life.

I continued to take care of my family and take my pills. After all, this was the 1960s. Being married had been like living in a time warp. The rest of the world was developing, while I'd been devolving. Other women were discovering liberation everywhere they looked, while I was discovering servitude. But now I looked around and, wow, had things changed! Women were speaking their minds, becoming political, chucking their bras. The whole country seemed to be smoking pot and listening to the Beatles. My next-door neighbor, Patti, was the original 1960s single chick—miniskirts, long hair, and knee-high boots—and she made the most of being a hip divorcée at a time when that word still had negative connotations. We didn't care. We were having too much fun.

Within three months after the operation I'd lost twenty pounds and before I knew it, I was dating the same three men I'd been seeing before my marriage, including Bob, the swinging salesman. The other divorcées told me that this wasn't unusual. "It's where you feel safe," they said.

More than ever before, Bob was into the drug scene which, although I was already taking prescription drugs, gave me an excuse to experiment further. It certainly wasn't hard to snag anything you wanted. Drugs were anywhere and everywhere—in the streets, in clubs, in your bathroom. They were as easy to come by as cigarettes, and just as socially acceptable. Above all, they helped me cope with the cancer scare and the divorce.

There was little doubt that being 26, divorced, and disillusioned in 1966 equaled trouble. But avoiding reality also has a price. The drugs allowed me to escape my helplessness, but that feeling never truly departed; the drugs were only camouflage, and it lay in wait, ready to return with a vengeance.

Throughout this period I had one strict rule: Never take a drug while the children were awake. I loved being a mother, and taking care of my girls was my pleasure and responsibility. I lived like a vampire, sleeping during the day while the kids took their naps; when they grew older, I would doze for hours while they were in school. I took drugs only when the girls were safely tucked into bed and fast asleep. I had no daytime privacy anyway, since my father liked to drop in unannounced with a cooked ham or some fresh fruit.

In the meantime, I gave no consideration to a career, or my finances, until one day Dad ordered me down to the bowling alley, threw a balled-up check at me, and said that my checks were bouncing all over town. Rather than make me learn how to balance the checkbook, he confiscated it. "I'm going to do it," he sighed, and from then on he just had me sign on the line after he wrote out the checks.

My life continued without discipline, direction, or discrimination. I was living the '60s to the max: free, loose, irresponsible, but also desperate and sad. I wasn't alone. Around me the entire scene was losing its golden aura. Too many drugs meant too much danger, and too much irresponsibility led to recklessness and stupidity. Janis Joplin said that freedom was just another word for nothing left to lose, but it was a lie. There was one other thing to lose, and that was your life. Slowly people were starting to die, among them some good friends. One was an accidental drug overdose, and two more committed suicide, including a man with whom I had fallen deeply in love.

Ed, who was married, was the same age as my father, which isn't a surprise, since they were friends. Charismatic and handsome, the head of entertainment at a Las Vegas casino, Ed immediately wanted to take care of me—what scent did I emit that caused men to make me this kind of offer so quickly? Perhaps it was an awareness that I would accept, as I did. Now I had both my father and Ed to lean on.

But once again I had fallen in love without looking. Our relationship quickly turned tempestuous because, although Ed swore that he loved me as he had never loved before, like most married men, he refused to leave his wife. I had entered into a dream world, pretending he was Mr. Right, all the while knowing in my heart that he was someone else's Mr. Right too. No matter how much Ed gave, I wanted more. Screaming fights erupted regularly, and soon we were in an ugly cycle of tumultuous breakups and precarious reconciliations.

Emotionally drained, Ed finally decided to stop seeing me, but to gain the strength to stick to this decision, he practically inhaled the contents of his bathroom medicine cabinet.

Not long afterward, in a dazed stupor, he called me to ask if we could talk things over in person. "We have to figure this thing out," he said. "I need to see you."

I agreed, but on the morning of my flight to Las Vegas, his secretary called to say that Ed had overdosed. It wasn't an accident. The last time I was able to tell him how much I loved him was at his funeral.

The message was beginning to sink in. It doesn't matter whether you dance around it, ignore it, thumb your nose at it, laugh at it, or pretend it's not there. Like it or not, reality is waiting for you.

My pain increased, and struggling to escape my darkness, I sought out a psychiatrist. He was the wrong man at the wrong time. Rather than deal with my suffering through conventional talk therapy, he injected me with sodium Pentothal, or truth serum, and recorded our conversations. He then asked me to listen to the tapes when I was alone.

The tapes' brutal honesty frightened me: All I heard was my own voice, droning on and on in dejection. I had suspected I was unhappy, but this abject despair was a shock and pushed me further into depression. (Not that this doctor himself was particularly healthy; he later checked himself into an institution to cure his own drug-abuse problem.)

My parents were too naive to consider the possibility that I was using drugs, but they suspected something was profoundly wrong. One day my mother came over, sat me down at the kitchen table, and said, "Judy, I don't know what's going on, but whatever it is, get it out of your system. Take some time off. I'll care for the kids until you figure this out."

That small speech accomplished what no therapy ever could. How far off the deep end must I have been for my mother to ask for my kids? I excused myself, went to the bathroom, looked at my reflection in the mirror, and said, "Do you really want to give your children to someone else? Are things that bad?"

I made a decision to survive. I drove over to my sister's apartment and said, "I have a drug problem."

Roni, who was in therapy, helped me find an excellent psychiatrist. But before he could say a word, I told him to get me into a hospital immediately because I was a drug abuser. I was so afraid, given my quick mind and mouth, that he'd be fooled by my intelligent facade.

Today, the willingness to admit to a substance-abuse problem generally means, among the well-to-do, a trip to a gracious, nurturing Betty Ford–type center filled with interesting people trying to shuck a bad habit. In the 1960s, drug and alcohol abusers were packed off to the same place as the mentally ill. A few days later I was checking myself into a hospital.

It was a strange new world. After taking away my belt and my hair dryer (I could strangle myself with the cord), they shunted me off to the intensive care unit, where I promptly fell asleep. But I woke up in the dark in the middle of the night and, terrified, asked the guard if he could find me a snack, which he did, and he then calmed me down.

I fell back asleep, but the next morning, when my roommate woke up and strapped on ancient army boots underneath her nightgown, I quickly remembered where I was.

The floor's first rule was that you couldn't stay inside your little bedroom, so I walked out into the large common area to get a sense of bearing. One look at my compatriots made me realize my psyche wasn't in such bad shape. Welcome to the Snake Pit, I thought. One boy stood in the corner, repeatedly banging his head against the wall, while an older woman dashed up and down the corridor, up and down, all day. Another girl continually curled her hair, uncurled it, and curled it, over and over. A Hollywood star who had just finished filming a movie about addiction checked in because, after making the movie, she realized she was an addict herself. One of my fellow inmates soon escaped by running down the hall, breaking down the door, and then leaping high over the fence. The hospital staff caught him at the bus stop across the street, where he was calmly waiting for a bus.

I felt comfortable among this odd group, because they seemed to understand me, which made me feel safe. One sweet young girl who played guitar and sang became my best friend, and we talked and smoked cigarettes for hours—we weren't allowed matches, but the guards were perfect gentlemen, lighting us up the moment we beckoned. As this was during an era when institutionalization had a romantic connotation—remember the movie *King of Hearts,* which convinced a generation of college students that only the insane were sane?—and we had long discussions about who was loony and who wasn't. The line between us and the staff seemed thin, at best.

A few days later they released me from intensive care and sent me off to an area where we were allowed to walk around freely. The resident therapist then took me aside and told me that I didn't belong at the hospital, because I admitted to abusing drugs, which meant I had reached a heightened level of self-awareness. Furthermore, he added, I had no real addictions.

"Nice try," I said. "I'm not going anywhere."

Why should I? Not only did I feel at ease with the people, the routine was comfortable. Someone made my bed, someone told me when to eat, someone gave me clothes to wear, someone told me when to sleep. I had no responsibilities. It was a completely entertaining life. We wove straw baskets, we made clay ashtrays, we listened to music, we talked, and we exercised in a little yard. I was sober and having fun being so. And, for the first time in my life, no one was saying, "Go find a husband to take care of you." They were saying, "You have to pull yourself up by your bootstraps. Take care of yourself. Own your problem."

And then, of course—the story of my life—I met a man: Robert, who had recently arrived for the same reasons I had. "Do you get it?" the doctor asked me, when I told him. "Do you see what you're doing? Do you really need a man in your life right now?"

But my vision was limited. All I saw was that Robert was gorgeous.

My mother was too upset with me to visit. My father, however, was concerned for my health in a new way. Whereas once he seemed concerned only with making me dependent on him, we now began to develop a real relationship. While my mother was saying, "How could you do this to me?," my father was saying, "Whatever it takes, we will help you, and we'll all do it together." I heard in those words his new commitment to help me reach some level of autonomy.

This faith helped me understand that I really could conquer my issues after all. Perhaps this was another reason I liked the hospital— I knew it was going to work. My head was becoming clear. One day my father looked at me and said, with surprise, "Your eyes! I can see your eyes again." I looked in the mirror and it was true: My eyes were no longer brown gashes beneath my eyebrows. They were wide again, and bright.

A month later the hospital gave me consent to leave, with the suggestion that I begin psychoanalysis, five days a week. I tackled that therapy as though it were the only life preserver in the ocean. Perhaps, for me, it was. For the first time, I started asking myself real questions. Why did I do drugs? Why did I keep looking for men? Above all, why did I feel so helpless and dependent?

I've spent the rest of my life trying to find answers to these as well as many other questions. No one resolves her life completely, but I know now that some of my issues concerned my feelings of powerlessness and uselessness. And some of the problem derived from my anger at my parents, for although devoted and well meaning, they'd contributed in the creation of this weak creature.

This was the knot I had to cut: Although in my thirties, I still clung to my father—or any other man—for support.

My psychoanalyst understood this. Deciding that part of my therapy concerned financial responsibility, he asked my father to help me learn to handle money. Perhaps, the doctor said, I could pay for the therapy myself, so that I'd feel the therapy was mine—even if the money came in the form of a family loan.

My father, with his new understanding of my needs, agreed; to accomplish it, he gave me a small piece of his bowling business, which he was currently selling, although staying on as chief operating officer. Dad and his partners called me in and asked me to sign a sheaf of papers, including an option agreement stating they could buy my piece out whenever they wished, and which I signed without understanding what I was doing, because they told me to.

Dad also wanted me to come in to work a few days a week, to give me some sense of involvement in the business. This was something like participating at a sanitarium work program—the attendance was more important than the labor. "Let's rebuild from the ground up," he said. "I'll teach you how money works."

"Sure," I said.

"Of course," he added, "you can bring your tennis racquet, and don't kill yourself. Just get your dad a cup of coffee now and then and see what goes on at an office."

Maybe it wasn't really work, but it was more than I'd done before. And, my father gave me back control of my checkbook.

So I started my job. I learned how to make coffee, how to order doughnuts, and how to greet people with a smile. I drew the line, however, when they asked me to use an adding machine. "I can't do that," I said. But they insisted I had to keep inventory of the liquor from the different bars, and within a few weeks I could work wonders with that machine. I realized that to master something, all you had to do was try it a few times, even if it involved something as frightening as numbers.

By this time one of my bosses had figured out I was smart and he decided I could do more. I agreed, and asked my father for his permission. If I had to be at the office, why not use my brain? I finally understood why women always wanted to quit their jobs and have babies. The men gave them nothing but menial tasks.

My father wasn't keen on my continuing education. "You're so smart," he kept saying, "if only you'd been a son." But he did permit me to attend bowling management school, where I was the only woman. I didn't care for it much. Perhaps this won't come as a surprise, but there's little to learn in bowling management school that applies to life in general.

Meanwhile, since owning a house was cheaper than renting, my father lent me $5,000 for a down payment on a nice three-bedroom home in Beverly Hills. My piece of the business was generating about $60,000 a year, which in the mid-1970s was very good money. I was a little bored at work, but I was happy. Life was good, which at this point meant stable.

It also meant that I was dating someone. During this period there was one steady man (a psychiatrist, but not mine, thank goodness). And my therapy was teaching me a good deal about my anger and self-destructiveness. I saw more clearly than ever how ill-prepared for life I was. And I understood I was blessed with some good traits, too, including an increasing amount of self-discipline. I once thought that if you wanted something, you went after it—instant gratification, no matter what the eventual cost. Now I was learning to think before acting.

Then, one sunny August afternoon in 1976, my father told me that he and my mother were going away for the weekend. "Good-bye, toots," he said, and flew off to Las Vegas, where a day later he was dead.

Chapter 5

Death, and Taxes

We don't pay taxes. Only the little people pay taxes.
Leona Helmsley

*T*hat last night in Las Vegas my parents went out to a nice dinner, lost a considerable amount of money shooting craps, and returned to their room, where they made love. A few minutes later my father fell to the floor with an embolism in his brain.

My mother was hysterical. Lou was the leader, not Fran. Lou knew what to do. Fran couldn't cope without direction. Confused and frightened, she ran out of the room into the hallway, but when she found it empty, she turned around and tried to reenter the room. She couldn't; she'd locked herself out. She then ran through the halls screaming, "He's dead! He's dead!"

That wasn't quite true; Lou was unconscious, hanging on to life by a slender thread, but by the time he was rushed to the hospital, his heart had given out too, and the thread snapped.

Lou's death had been too quick for him to feel a thing; unfortunately, for my mother, the pain was devastating. On the phone, trying to tell me what had happened, her sobbing made her voice incomprehensible. "What?" I kept asking.

"Daddy's dead," she finally blurted out.

I quickly called my sister, who couldn't handle it. "Not my dad," she said. "Nope. Not my dad." I realized I should never have told her over the phone.

When my brother Gary and I arrived in Las Vegas, my mother was still wearing her nightgown, and she refused to take a shower or change because they had made love just before he died; she didn't want to lose that closeness. We had to take her home in the gown.

She couldn't stop crying. "I can't live alone," she screamed. "I can't do anything. I can't make it."

"Come live with me," I said, and she did. I moved into Audrey's room, and my mother moved into mine.

Once we had finally calmed her down, Oscar, my father's best friend and lawyer, told us that he would handle everything. "Nothing to worry about," he said. "There's plenty of money. It's a little complicated, but everything's under control." And he warned us to get into Dad's safe-deposit box before the IRS did, because he guessed that Dad had stockpiled a great deal of cash there.

Meanwhile, Dad's strongbox at home turned out to be empty, which was an unpleasant surprise, as was the discovery that he had only $18,000 in his checking account. So now we knew all the money had to be in that safe-deposit box. But when we opened it, all we found were my grandparents' birth certificates, a couple of old wills, and a large pile of empty rubber bands that had once held rolls of cash.

We ransacked the house. Nothing. We scoured his office. Nothing. We knew he was a millionaire. Where were the millions?

Sorting through all my father's belongings, I soon found not stocks or cash or bonds, but Las Vegas markers. We had all known that my father was a gambler, but we'd never grasped the extent of it. Now I found canceled checks to casinos for big, crazy numbers: $150,000, $65,000, $200,000. Apparently he loved those craps tables. I remembered that whenever he gambled, some lackey would follow him around with a chair, so he could sit whenever he wanted. "That was the most expensive chair in America," I now told my sister. "It cost us our inheritance."

I asked Oscar point blank where the money was. "I was supposed to be an heiress," I said. "We lived without worry. Did he do it with smoke and mirrors?"

"Not to worry," Oscar said. "Everything will be fine, just fine." His deep, masculine voice reassured us all. Just fine, we thought. Still, there was no money.

Meanwhile, I found among my father's papers evidence that he'd borrowed a good deal of money from relatives. I also discovered the deed to my house, which wasn't even in my name.

"Not to worry," Oscar said. "I have another deed, and that one certainly is in your name." He promised to sort out all these problems, giving us our only sense of security. One night I said to my mother, "Thank God for Oscar."

The following morning he died of a heart attack.

Under normal circumstances, this would have been cause for a round of hysterics, but I didn't have the time to break down, not with my mother demanding that I take charge, all the while refusing to exit my bedroom.

Searching through more papers, I found a series of notes indicating that my father owed his partners even more money than we'd thought and, curiously enough, notes saying that they owed him money, too. Desperate, I sought out a friend who was wealthy and smart. But as soon as he realized what these notes meant, he froze. "Don't show me anything else," he said. "This is privileged information." He sent me to a lawyer, who in turn instructed me to involve Allen, Oscar's former partner.

So, a few days later, my sister and I went in to see Allen, a sensible, solid man, who, after listening to our story, reassured us that he could help. Then, when the meeting ended, he asked me to dinner.

Diana

Diana, a 41-year-old lawyer, has never married. Working in-house for a midsize corporation for more than a dozen years, she makes $150,000 a year. She has a wonderful $500,000 condominium, with a mortgage of about $250,000. Through her job, she has good life and health insurance, but no pension plan.

In addition to an IRA of $25,000, Diana has saved $100,000.

However, she has put all this money into long-term CDs paying 6 percent interest, and has divided the pot into two banks to guarantee that each account is fully FDIC insured. Diana is convinced the economy could crash at any minute, and she wants to be as safe as possible. In other words, although Diana is quite intelligent, she's financially risk-averse, and she hasn't taken advice very well. Her last planner couldn't convince her to do anything at all to grow her money, and she fired him.

During our discussion, I found that some of Diana's moves were smart. Over the last decade she had accumulated her $100,000 by carefully saving $500 every month, according to what I call the pay-yourself-first plan: Before she spent a penny, she put her $500 in the bank. Then, at the end of the month, if she had money left over, she put that away, too. Not that her budget didn't allow her clothes, a nice car, and an occasional vacation to Europe. But she always took care of her savings account first.

Diana also knew her work-related insurance policy inside and out, especially disability and health, because she's hyperglycemic, and her medical needs will increase over time.

I told Diana that a problem was brewing. "You've grown accustomed to a certain life-style," I said. "But you're not doing anything to guarantee that you can continue living like that once you retire." Given how Diana was investing her money, she was barely keeping up with inflation.

Since she didn't understand, I went over the numbers for her, as I had for Marcy. Diana is making 6 percent interest on her CDs. Her total tax bill takes out 2.2 percentage points of that money. That leaves her with 3.8 percent after taxes. If inflation on average is currently 3 percent, that leaves Diana with a profit of .8 percent.

"You'll never be able to stop working that way," I said. "Not if you want to live as you do now."

"But I've looked at charts comparing people my age," Diana said. "I've saved a good amount of money."

"True," I agreed. "You've done a good job saving your money. The problem is where you've invested it."

Diana seemed to understand this, but she didn't want to hear about risk. "I'm afraid that if I put my money someplace where it isn't insured, I'm going to lose it all."

"Why?" I asked.

"I'm just afraid," she said. I then showed Diana scenarios with her money invested at different rates of return. And I reminded her that everyone takes risks in life, all the time. For instance, Diana was taking several prescriptions for her hyperglycemia. "Every time you put a drug into your body you're ingesting something you know almost nothing about," I said. "You're trusting your doctor and the research that's been done on that drug. Markets are unknown to you too, but here you can also trust a professional and the research that's gone into investment advice. Neither medicine nor investing is foolproof, but if done properly, you can minimize the risk in each one."

I also recommended that Diana could afford a bigger mortgage. "It's your only good tax deduction," I said. Again, the small mortgage showed Diana's natural conservative streak at play; she was trying to pay off her debt. But in a low-interest environment, this doesn't make sense. Diana could obtain a loan for 7.5 percent, and use the tax break on her interest payments for other purposes.

"Increase your mortgage to seventy percent of the value of your home," I said, "and add it to the one hundred thousand dollars. That will give you another one hundred thousand dollars. Now you have two hundred thousand dollars to invest—plus the money in your IRA. At your age, you need growth. You don't want to end up with two hundred thousand dollars. You want much more."

We went over how much money she needed to retire.

"Let's say you'll need ninety-two thousand dollars a year when you retire," I said. "By the time you're sixty-five, assuming a 3 percent inflation rate over these next two decades, that means you'll really need a little over one hundred ninety-two thousand, five hundred dollars a year. So we really have to grow that money of yours."

I recommended the following portfolio for Diana: Her $25,000 IRA was where she could take the most risk, since she wasn't going to touch it for a quarter of a century. So this money went into growth stocks.

She also needed some cash as an emergency fund—three months' expenses, or about $25,000—so I proposed leaving that much in CDs.

I then suggested that 60 percent of the balance of her portfolio go into growth: meaning, a diversified portfolio of small and large company stocks. On the income side—40 percent of her portfolio—I recommended she use some intermediate-term municipal bonds and place a small amount into high-yield corporate bonds.

Investors with large amounts of money should consider the tax consequences, which is why investments such as municipal bonds can be valuable: They're exempt from federal taxes, as well as from state taxes, if you live in the state in which they were issued. Their return is adjusted for this savings—i.e., they don't pay as much interest as other bonds, but for people in high tax brackets, the tax savings can be helpful.

Diana took the advice, although withdrawing her CDs wasn't easy for her. But she was too smart to ignore the facts; she understands that her life-style will suffer tomorrow if she doesn't invest today.

◆ ◆ ◆

*H*ere was my life, all over again: Go to the lawyer for help, and end up going out with the lawyer. It wasn't long before I was truly, madly, deeply in love. Allen, thirteen years older, bright, calm, and ethical, stepped in and took over where my father had left off. I loved him so much I now wondered if I'd ever truly loved before.

At first Allen attended to matters related to my father's estate, but he soon became increasingly involved in all of our lives as we uncovered my father's dealings—and he had some very strange dealings indeed. It went without saying (and yet we couldn't stop saying it) that my father was not the Goody Two-shoes who had walked through snow and sleet to get straight As that he had portrayed himself to be.

For instance, Oscar had told me not to concern myself about that house deed, because he had a "better deed" at the office. When Allen looked at that last one closely, he discovered that it was signed and dated 1974. However, the actual deed form wasn't printed until 1976.

My father and Oscar had created a phony deed and backdated it. I didn't own my house after all.

I also discovered notes in his files for as much as $300,000, evidence that my father and various associates had been playing all kinds of tax games, loaning one another vast sums to avoid tax payments. And we found more evidence of enormous gambling debts. Soon calls were coming in from all over Las Vegas, trying to collect. But we never paid a single casino a cent. How could we? There was no money.

Only one casino pressed us. "Your father left with our money," the caller said.

"He left dead," I replied.

"It was the trip before."

"Mom's in shock," I said. "So am I. We don't have the money to pay you. Anyway, you already have everything Dad ever made."

Eventually they left us alone. God knows how much money my father lost in Vegas. I'm sure he added his own wing to Caesar's Palace. If Dad had been paying more attention to his finances, and less to the craps table, all of us would have been much better off. And we would have been even more so, if he hadn't tried skirting some of his taxes.

Taxes

Boy, was Leona Helmsley ever wrong about paying taxes. Everyone pays taxes. If you don't, you go to jail. Leona did. It's that simple. My father fooled around with his taxes, and look at the mess he left us.

In America, we're taxed on practically everything financial: what we earn, what we give away, what we buy, what we leave behind when we die, and so on. In other words, you can run, but you can't hide. Back in 1789 Benjamin Franklin said that "nothing is certain but death and taxes," but my sense is that you'd have an easier time avoiding death.

Yet all in all, the American taxation system is pretty fair. Those of us who have should take care of those who have not. I gladly give my fifty cents on every dollar, hoping it will go to the sick, the helpless, and the homeless. But it doesn't. Much of my tax money goes to those good-ol'-boy politicians flying around in their private jets and playing with their war toys. But the government doesn't let me or anyone else decide where tax dollars go and so, although I resent my money being wasted, I can't do anything about it. We all pay, and we might as well take pride in the good our tax dollars do and ignore the rest.

How do you best plan for taxes? The bottom line is: Simply don't spend the part of your income that's going to be taxed. Be realistic. If you have a full-time job, your employer deducts taxes every week or two, so there shouldn't be any surprises at the end of the year. And if you're self-employed, you're paying taxes quarterly (or you should be), so pay attention. Why spend what you don't have? And yet I've found that, much more often than men, women fail to focus on the taxable part of their income when preparing their budgets. They think more in terms of *gross* income rather than *net*—gross is your money before you've paid taxes, and net is what's left afterward.

Try to think in terms of real money. It's nice to have the self-image of someone who makes $100,000 a year, but don't go out and spend all that money. With that kind of income, you may be bringing in only around $65,000 after federal, state, and local taxes, as well as Social Security and any other taxes you incur. Be careful. If you spend what you don't have, you'll have more than taxes to worry about.

◆ ◆ ◆

The most important step in doing your taxes: finding a good tax adviser to help you. Unless you're able to use the short form knowledgeably, or you're that singular person who understands tax rules, consider hiring an expert. More than half the U.S. population now does.

Perhaps adviser is the wrong word, because there's only so much advice anyone can give you: If you're on salary, the routine is that each week or two you take your paycheck and the employer pays your tax, you take another paycheck, the employer again pays your tax, and so on. If you're on your own, then you pay estimated taxes quarterly. But you do need someone to help you file taxes properly.

The tax laws are not only complicated, but they change constantly, as they just did in the summer of 1997. The person you choose to prepare your taxes should be someone who stays well informed of tax developments. At the very least, she should be educated as an accountant, with several years' experience as a full- or part-time tax accountant.

There are some advantages to hiring a CPA (a certified public accountant): This person is licensed, has passed a national exam, and must maintain her education yearly. And the licensing bodies in each state, as well as CPA professional societies, offer disciplinary measures for those who don't maintain standards.

I also recommend tax experts who are known as "enrolled agents," which means they've been certified by the IRS to prepare taxes.

Your tax adviser must not only be intelligent, she should have the smarts to ask you the right questions. For instance, it's likely that you won't know what papers and records to bring with you, so you'll need someone who's good at soliciting that information.

When you find someone you like, have her prepare engagement letters that set out the scope of your relationship. Put down in writing that your CPA will prepare your 1040 form for this year for such-and-such a price, and other provisions, such as how you arrived at the price, and what happens if you don't pay. This is for your protection, and when dealing with money, protection is always important. Then again, it's important in other areas of your life, too.

If you don't have a good adviser, don't run out and find one in the Yellow Pages. Ask a friend whose financial affairs seem to be well run for a recommendation. Listen to her when she talks about her taxes— does she seem knowledgeable about the advantages of things like leasing a car or selling a house? If so, she may be the person to consult for a referral.

And if you move to a new town where you don't know a soul, you can always call the state society of CPAs for a recommendation.

But don't look for a tax adviser based on how little tax she claims she can "arrange" for you to pay. Likewise, when you first meet with a new adviser, make sure she doesn't wink and poke and insinuate the "funny" things she might be able to do. If you don't think she's on the level, leave. Why? Because when completing your tax returns, the cardinal, primary, principal, elemental, fundamental, ultimate rule is: Be honest.

Always live by the rules. And not just because you might get caught. Honesty makes your whole life easier. You don't have to worry later, you don't have to sweat over the outcome should you be audited, you can sleep at night. Pay your fair share and forget about it.

A word of warning to all wives who sign joint returns: The fact that you don't read the form your husband and/or his advisers prepare for you doesn't mean that you're not liable for any transgressions. By signing that tax document, you're agreeing that, if there's a deficiency, both you and your spouse are accountable, and if your spouse can't come up with the money, it's your responsibility to do so.

Let's say you're married, and your husband Harry has been making a great living, and he's been doing everything and anything for you, including preparing your taxes. And so every year he says, "Becky, sign here." All you look at is the signature page, and you sign. Do you know what you're signing? No. You sign all those forms because you trust Harry. Do you care? No. Should you care? Yes. What happens if next year Harry leaves you for his 24-year-old secretary? It's hello, Rachel; good-bye, Becky. You also trusted him not to run off. And now it's a year later and you're looking at a letter from the IRS saying, "Becky, we're auditing you." You think, This is Harry's problem. No, it's not, Becky. It's yours. Maybe Harry's broke now because Rachel ran away with all his money, and he can't pay a dime—it doesn't matter. *You* still owe money to the IRS.

My friend Marta knew her husband was cheating the IRS for years. He always told her, "Hey, the government screws us, so why shouldn't we screw them?" She agreed, and year after year she signed return after return saying that her husband made $75,000, instead of the $175,000 he really earned. The couple used that extra cash to pay for food, clothing, and anything else they could get away with—plenty of people out there love you to pay them in cash. Then disaster hit. Life's a round wheel after all. The husband sued for divorce and Marta took him to court to fight over support. "We made $175,000," she said. But the judge said, "No, you didn't. You signed these tax returns saying you made $75,000." Marta was screwed. If she turned in her hubby, she was turning herself in, too. So she lost on her alimony and child support what she made on the tax savings.

(Yes, there are **innocent spouse provisions,** meaning that if you, as a wife, didn't understand what you were doing when you signed that dishonest return, you might not be penalized. But it's difficult to qualify for these provisions. You have to be truly removed from what's going on, and have no reason to know there was a substantial under-statement when you signed your name. Few people are that out of it. Stupidity is not a defense.)

I have no sympathy for cheaters. I pay my taxes and I don't want someone else successfully avoiding them. We should all kiss the earth every day that we live in this country and can afford to pay our taxes instead of receiving the goodwill from them. But, God forbid, it's great that this country will try to help us if we ever need it.

Report all your income. Period.

There is, however, a little more room on the deduction side. Here you should be more aggressive than the IRS, which is always at point zero: In other words, they'll always interpret the law in black and white, and try to give you no leeway. But the law isn't actually written that way, and that's why there are so many books about preparing taxes.

The IRS has limited patience with people who don't report income. They get nasty. Let's say that you receive a notice to meet with IRS agent Joan. If Joan discovers a consistent pattern in your failure to report all your income, then all of Joan's alarm bells go off, and the next thing you know, you're in a full-blown examination of all your records. Agents are never comfortable when they discover unreported income.

But Joan is much less likely to press penalties to the max if she simply disagrees with some of your deductions, which are often gray and arguable.

It's unlikely, however, that you'll go to prison no matter what you do, unless you're really a crook. In a criminal case, the government has to prove that you intentionally tried to defraud the government. The civil side of tax law works differently, however, and may be the only part of U.S. law where you're more or less guilty until you prove yourself innocent. In other words: You're liable for your taxes unless you can prove otherwise. If Joan says this deduction is no good, you have to prove to her that it is.

All of this means that you must keep good records. By doing so, over the course of the year you'll accumulate all proof of income and deductions. For example, keep a careful checkbook, indicating what's coming in and going out. Retain copies of individual records, such as tax returns and bank statements, for six years after filing. Other records, including property titles and accountant's audit reports, should be kept permanently. If you're not sure how long to hold on to papers, the IRS will send you a sheet detailing which items must be retained, and for how long.

The more meticulous your records, the easier it will be for your tax adviser to accumulate data for tax returns, and the lower your cost to have your returns prepared.

◆ ◆ ◆

Below are a few basic tax facts often asked about by women. No one says that you have to be an expert on taxes. But if you choose to read the following information, try to absorb enough so that when your taxes are next prepared, you can be a little more prepared, also.

The first area we'll discuss is filing status. Here, you have several options.

If you're married, you can file either a **joint return** with your spouse, or you can file as **married, filing separately.** If you file the latter form, you must be careful how you allocate your income between you and your spouse; there are also special rules for married individuals living in community-property states like California.

If you're unmarried, there are three categories of filing status. The first category is **single.** The second is **unmarried, head of household;** to qualify for it, you must maintain a household for an unmarried child. This rate is more favorable than that for filing as single. The third category is **qualifying widow.** This filing status is available for the next two years following the year in which a spouse dies, if you have a child living at home. This tax rate is also more favorable than that for filing as single.

Filing status is determined on the last day of the year: That is, if you get divorced on December 31, you're considered single for the entire year. Conversely, if you get married on December 31, you're treated as being married for the entire year. But don't use this information to try to fool the IRS. If you divorce on December 31 and remarry on January 1, you're still considered married for the years in question. They're not dopes. (And do you really want to marry that guy who's divorcing and remarrying you as a tax dodge? Get a new boyfriend!)

Another thing to keep in mind throughout the year is: Just exactly what income is taxable?

The tax return itself presents you with categories of taxable income; **capital gains,** for example. Capital gains are transactions whereby you buy and sell an asset, such as a house, resulting in a profit or loss. Furthermore, certain kinds of income, or **receipts,** *aren't* taxable. For example, interest from certain bonds isn't a taxable receipt. Gifts, such as a present from a friend, aren't taxable income (but if the gift is larger than $10,000 per year, then gift taxes may be due). However, these gift taxes are usually paid by the donor—see the section on estate planning, page 84.

If you're receiving a pension of any sort as a result of your spouse's death or divorce, a portion of that money is taxable. So even though your spouse may have put away a million dollars in a pension plan, and that value is included in his estate, it doesn't mean that you can receive it without paying income tax.

A portion of Social Security benefits is generally taxable. Alimony can be taxable, depending on the divorce documents. (Child support is not taxable income under any circumstances.)

A good rule of thumb is that amounts you receive are taxable if they're tax deductions to whomever paid you. If you borrow money, and you pay interest on it, sometimes that interest is deductible; the flip side is that the recipient gets taxable interest income.

The income side of what is and is not taxable is simpler than the deduction side. So pay close attention to the next area: What is deductible?

If expenses are business-related, they're usually deductible. Business deductions include any kind of expenses you incur in operating your business (that is, if you're the sole proprietor).

Hobby expenses aren't deductible. The difference between a hobby and a business is that the latter is an activity engaged in for profit, and so you must have a reasonable expectation that you will make a profit (whether or not you actually make any money isn't key—and believe me, many people go through several years where they don't). Otherwise, that little stamp collection of yours is a hobby, and the expenses of maintaining it aren't deductible.

Many non-business expenses are also deductible: medical expenses, for instance, provided they exceed a certain threshold based on how much income you earn. (It's not just your doctor bills that are deductible—contact lenses are deductible; so is parking at the doctor's office, as are contraceptives, if bought with a prescription.) This threshold is high, however: As of 1996, it stood at 7.5 percent of your adjusted gross income, or your income before taking either the standard deduction or itemizing.

Taxes, such as state income taxes and real-estate property taxes, are generally deductible. Sales taxes are not deductible.

Mortgage interest on your principal residence and one other residence is usually deductible with some limitations, one being that the underlying debt cannot exceed $1,100,000 (you should be so unlucky). Interest on credit cards, personal car loans, and other loans of a personal nature isn't deductible. However, if you pay interest on an auto loan for a vehicle that is used for business, then at least some deductions are available.

Contributions to charity are deductible if the charitable organization is qualified as such by the IRS. The contribution doesn't have to be cash, although keep in mind that the deductible value of a non-cash contribution is the property's fair market value, not what you paid for it. For example, say you bought 100 shares of stock for $1,000 and now they're worth $5,000; if you give those 100 shares to charity, you get a $5,000 contribution deduction. But clothes given away to a thrift shop qualify as a charitable contribution equal to their fair market price, which is usually less than their original cost, since they're used.

Another category of deductions is casualty and theft losses. But again, these deductions have to exceed a threshold based on your income; the more you earn, the bigger the casualty loss has to be before you can deduct it.

One other category of deductions worth mentioning is miscellaneous deductions (which also have to exceed certain thresholds), including investment advisory fees, legal and accounting fees, tax-return preparation fees, safekeeping fees, and gambling losses to the extent of gambling winnings—i.e., the losses can't exceed gambling winnings. (There's a famous case of a guy who won a lot of money at the track and, after claiming a substantial gambling loss, was audited. When asked to produce support for all his losses, the man showed the IRS agent hundreds of losing tickets—the agent thought it was terrific he had so much support, but he questioned why all the tickets were covered with footprints.)

The most important thing to keep in mind concerning deductions: Don't overlook any. Make sure every penny you've laid out during the year that's deductible shows up on your tax form.

Something else to remember is the difference between earnings made as an employee and those made as an independent contractor.

Here the distinction concerns control: Who controls your hours, what you do, and the tools you use? If the person you're working for is in control, then you're an employee. Therefore, your employer is required to withhold money from your salary; the employer, in effect, pays your income taxes. However, if you aren't controlled by the person for whom you're working (say you're a writer who owns her own computer, sets her own hours, and takes assignments with various people) then you're an independent contractor. If you're an independent contractor, the person or people for whom you work don't withhold, or pay Social Security taxes, and thus you have to pay your own taxes, and must do so on a quarterly basis. In addition, these quarterly payments, or estimated taxes, have to be paid on other income that's not earned income, such as dividends, alimony, etc.

If you're self-employed, you must also pay self-employment taxes, which at the moment exceed 15 percent of the income from that activity, separate from income taxes.

There are other miscellaneous taxes, such as the notorious Nanny Tax, which you should know about in case you employ a domestic in your home (particularly if you want to be nominated for U.S. attorney general), and excise taxes, which must be paid if you pull out too much money from a pension plan in a particular year.

◆ ◆ ◆

If your tax planner is good, after helping you with income and deductions, she can also help you assess your spending habits by telling you how much you have left for expenditures on an after-tax basis. She can also figure out, based on your annual receipts and disbursements, how much you have available to save. She can even create a spreadsheet showing where all your money has gone over a six-month period. This can help you reduce your spending habits by unearthing categories that you might have otherwise forgotten.

Use your tax adviser to make the most of your income. Like any other professional, she's there to help. If she doesn't help, fire her. It's that easy. So ask questions. Get answers. Be a part of the process.

◆ ◆ ◆

A few tips:

- If the tax-preparation fees in your area are too expensive, try one of the national storefront chains, such as H&R Block, or Beneficial Income Tax Service. They're very reasonable—the average fee is around $60.
- As we will discuss in the section on retirement, the government gives you few areas where you can make money tax-free, such as

a 401(k), an IRA, or a Keogh plan. Take advantage of every tax break you can find, including these.

- Act like a Girl Scout, and be prepared. Even if you're not currently involved in your financial affairs, you must still organize your own papers. Keep track of everything, such as your will, your husband's will, any trusts you or he owns, insurance policies, etc. When you go to your tax preparer, you'll save time if you bring in everything you need.
- If you know that you're owed a refund, file early. You'll get your refund earlier, and whom would you rather have earning interest income, the government or yourself?
- Coordinate your tax planning with estate planning, investment planning, and retirement planning. All these areas work together: if you do badly in one area, it will affect all the others.
- If you need to, you can extend your tax deadline for filing your return. But be sure you fill out the correct request forms. Ask your tax preparer for help.
- If you prepare your own taxes and own a computer, there's some excellent software available to help you. Try TurboTax or Mac-Intax.
- Pay your mortgage on time, or even a month early, to receive an extra month's interest expense deduction.
- If you do free-lance work at home, ask your preparer to see if you qualify for a home-office deduction. The IRS has stiffened the rules in this area, but it's always worth checking.
- Don't forget that each individual can give someone a gift of up to $10,000 every year without paying taxes on it. A couple can give $20,000 a year to each of their children, for instance. This rule can help you save on estate taxes. (See the section on estate planning, page 84.)
- The IRS publishes dozens of pamphlets to help you understand their rules and your obligations. You can order them by calling (800) TAX-FORM (that's 829-3676). They also have a Web site: http://www.irs.ustreas.gov/basic/cover/html.

Chapter 6

Still More Death, and Planning Wisely for It

To die will be an awfully big adventure.

J. M. Barrie

he Great Provider in life, Dad, turned out to be not such a great provider in death.

He had an addiction: gambling. It was a disease. Because of it, rather than leaving us a fortune, he ended up leaving us in the dark. He'd been earning more than $350,000 a year and had sold his business for a large sum the year before he died. Now, when all was tallied up, Mom realized about $60,000 from one small life-insurance policy, plus she still had equity in her condo, and owned a building that was paying out $36,000 a year. And I still had my 5 percent of the business.

From the taken-care-of to the caretaker: I was now my mother's guardian. I was finally forced to manage a checkbook, pay bills, and, God forbid, manage money. My mother once called me Lou. She turned to me and said, "You have to do this for me, Lou."

So I learned. I dealt with the casinos. I dealt with the debts. I dealt with whatever income we found. Basically, we had enough to live comfortably.

And I was so in love with my new man that I was fantasizing about marriage. But Allen had no intention of tying any knots, which wounded me so deeply I decided to leave Los Angeles.

My first thought was Hawaii, but my mother felt that was too far, so I ended up in Newport Beach, fifty miles south of Los Angeles, where

I knew no one. A real-estate broker found me a pretty little house, and I settled in for what I hoped would be an uneventful period in my life.

Laura

Like myself at that point in my life, Laura, who's 47, had never held a real job. Her husband Hal had always made a good salary, and both of them decided when they married that Laura would stay home and take care of their kids. But Hal died unexpectedly of a heart attack a few months ago at the age of 55, and now Laura's on her own.

Laura was lucky that Hal was a caring, responsible provider, both in life and in death. He left her an estate through a will and a living trust worth $1,150,000: $750,000 in cash and securities, including $250,000 from various life-insurance policies, plus a $500,000 house which is 80 percent paid for, giving her $400,000 of equity.

Laura has no desire to start a career; she'd rather continue volunteering at the museum she'd started working at when the kids, now 19 and 20, went off to college—both to state schools, so the bills are minimal. Hal always took all the financial responsibility for the family and never shared any information about it. I told Laura how fortunate she was that Hal turned out to be so reliable—she really had no idea what was in store for her when he died. Plenty of widows who were once as complacent as Laura have woken to find that no one had been doing any planning, and as a result they faced grave economic uncertainty.

Laura, who doesn't like talking about finances, would prefer someone else to take care of everything, yet she knows something has to be done with her inheritance.

Basically, Laura's in good shape. As a spouse, her inheritance passes to her estate tax-free. "This is a nice sum," I said, but we still have to be careful, since Laura doesn't intend to add to it during her lifetime.

We then worked on her cash flow, and discovered that Laura was living on $80,000 a year, which is more than she can expect to make from her $750,000, because even if she made an excellent 12 percent, bringing her $90,000 a year, after taxes she'd only have somewhere around $65,000.

Laura had three possibilities. The first was to try and grow her $750,000 by making some more aggressive investments. The second plan would be to slash Laura's budget by more than $15,000. She might easily discover that there are certain items on her budget no longer necessary now that Hal is gone.

The third choice was to sell the house, which tied up a good deal of her money. "Do you really need it," I asked, "now that the kids are no longer living at home?"

Laura admitted that she didn't, but she also didn't feel she could let go of it so soon after Hal's death—she considered the house one of the few stable elements in her life. Also, she wanted to give her younger child, a sophomore, the opportunity to spend vacations at home until she graduated.

I still recommended that Laura consider selling the house eventually, which could help close the gap.

Laura promised that she would consider this, but first she wanted to see if she could economize by paring her budget. For instance, Hal had insisted on maintaining two expensive cars, but Laura would be just as happy selling both and buying a more economical car. She also decided she could do without expensive vacations, since she felt reluctant to go off on her own now.

In investing Laura's money I recommended a conservative approach. After setting aside $50,000 for her immediate cash needs, I recommended Laura put 75 percent of her money into bonds for income, and 25 percent into stocks for growth. The fixed-income portfolio was divided between intermediate-term municipal bonds, U.S. corporate bonds, some high-yield corporate bonds, and short-term Treasuries for liquidity. The growth side was divided between large cap and growth stocks.

I felt Laura should use a professional money manager because, at her level of assets, the fees will be reasonable in relationship to her account. Furthermore, she wasn't interested in developing her financial acumen.

And, as with Marcy, I recommended Laura see an estate planner to get a new will and a living trust in place as soon as possible, since she had considerable assets that she needed to protect if she wanted to pass them along to her children.

◆ ◆ ◆

*M*y life just wasn't meant to be uneventful.

Over the last few years, my younger sister, Roni, had been running a well-known local jeweler's concession. Now she wanted to launch her own business, so she started looking at new lines, including one in San Diego.

One early September morning in 1978, Roni and my mother went down to meet Roni's contact. I remember that day vividly: I was sitting by my pool, watching television, feeling grateful that peace had entered my life, when a newscaster interrupted the regular programming to announce that a plane had just crashed near San Diego, with no survivors.

I knew my sister and mother were driving south, so I wasn't worried.

A few minutes later, my uncle Leon called. "Did your mother drive or fly to San Diego?" he asked.

"How could you think such a horrible thought?" I said, and slammed the receiver down. My body suddenly felt cold and without understanding how I knew, I knew my sister and mother were dead.

I called Allen. "I have this horrible premonition they were on the plane," I said.

"Who?" he asked. "What?"

I explained, and he promised to find out. A few minutes later he called back. "It's the worst," he said.

They say every life is a song of various melodies, some sad, some joyous, some beautiful. Mine was stuck on the same miserable tune. Just as I was coming up for air after my father's death and Allen's rejection, I plunged back into emotional paralysis. I stopped eating. I stopped socializing. I stopped sleeping. I stopped. Only Allen and my friend Chris could penetrate my unhappiness, and if they hadn't supervised my every move, I don't know what would have happened. I was a zombie. Not even a walking zombie, because for most of the time I refused to move. I sat and stared at the walls. Sometimes, for variety, I stared at the ceiling.

September passed into October, but it was all the same to me.

October passed into November, and I still couldn't move. Nor could I sleep well, but when I did sleep, nightmares tortured me. My sister saturated my dreams—she was a fetus, she was a corpse, she was dying, she was in trouble. In one dream, I was lying on the airplane nose, pounding on the window, trying to grab the pilot's attention to tell him he was going to crash. "Stop!" I howled. He couldn't hear. I woke up screaming.

It was only for the kids' sake that I was able to break out of my depression. I had to. I knew that if I didn't find a way to grab hold, my life would end, and my kids would be alone. But how? Already conditioned to look to therapy for help, I decided to find a psychiatrist, and ran into some real luck: Dr. Justin Call, a genuinely wise man. "Please," I begged him, "help me make something positive out of this mess I call my life."

He did. First, he forced me to move—literally. "Get out of the house," he said. "Walk someplace. Do something physical." And so I did, and discovered endorphins.

Then Dr. Call urged me to work on my grieving. The need to mourn was so tremendous, and I surrendered to it; all I did was cry and grieve, grieve and cry, cry and grieve, and worry about my kids. Standing in the shower with the water turned up full steam, I would sob my heart out, thinking that the girls couldn't hear my moans, but years later Stacey told me they'd penetrated the entire house.

After several months of grief, I began to regain some perspective and, taking stock of my life, trying to look toward the light rather than the dark, I realized I still had my kids, my health, and enough money to take care of us all. Perhaps there was some hope.

Perhaps not.

On the first morning I felt strong enough to take a walk, I found a registered letter from my father's partners lying in my post-office box.

I knew something was wrong. Trembling, I opened it.

The partners were exercising their option to buy out my shares of the business.

I froze. This spelled trouble—but that's all I knew; I wasn't much of a financial speller yet. I called Allen. "Can they do this?" I asked. The partners were offering me $125,000 for my share. That $125,000 share had been earning me $65,000 a year. Even I knew that $125,000 invested at 10 percent was only $12,500, or more than $50,000 less than what I'd been making.

"I don't know," he said.

After investigating the issue, Allen discovered that I had, indeed, signed the option—that paper I'd never bothered to read because my father and his partners had told me to sign it.

"They want you out and they'll find a way," Allen said. "But this isn't a fair price, so don't sell yet. We'll fight."

Soon afterward I was served at my front door with a notice; the partners were suing me, claiming that I'd signed the option but had never intended to sell my shares. I was still languishing in such depression that, on my own, I probably would have folded. "Goodbye, world," I would have said, and disappeared forever into the woodwork.

Luckily, Allen offered to fight for me. "But I can't afford you," I said. "I'll end up owing you the entire $125,000."

"It's a present," he promised. Without that, I wouldn't have made it.

The partners stopped paying me while we were at war, which reduced my income 100 percent. Now I was desperate. If only my father had planned for his death more wisely. And if only my mother, whom I loved so dearly, could have had the time between his death and hers to learn how to prepare her estate properly, perhaps the situation wouldn't have been so bleak. Think about it: You must begin to prepare for death before it happens. What's the alternative?

21 Questions on Estate Planning

1. Why is estate planning important?

I teach women to pay attention to their finances throughout their lives—and after their lives, too. Do you want to pay more taxes than necessary? Do you want relatives fighting over your money? Wouldn't you like to help charities you admire, and receive tax benefits from doing so?

Why not be as careful with your money after your life is over as you are during it? That is, if you have any money to leave behind. I don't mean to be an alarmist, because the odds are very much against this happening to you, but anyone can die at any moment. Why not be ready, just in case?

If you don't take care of your estate planning with a proper will, you'll have no control over your assets after your death, and everything will go through intestate succession laws, which vary from state to state. (If you die without a will, you have died *intestate*.) In some states, all community property goes to your spouse, not your children —or, if it's your separate property, it may be divided half to the child, half to the spouse; or, if you have two kids, it could go two-thirds to the children, and one-third to the spouse. None of this may be what you had in mind.

So think about your life, and your death. You can't take it with you, but you can make sure that others don't take it, either.

2. What do I want to accomplish with my estate plan?

In some ways, this is the key question.

By planning your estate carefully, you learn more about your own priorities. Who is important to you? What are your values? Do you want to give money to your relatives, or to charities? Estate planning forces you to look at your life, and this can be an excellent form of self-reflection.

You also want to think about how best to help others. There may be a number of ways to work with, say, your parents. If you want to leave them money, it might make sense to leave it in a trust, rather than as an outright bequest. This way, you can help your parents, yet prevent this money from being subject to tax in their estates. Each of your heirs will benefit from a thoughtful approach to his or her inheritance.

3. But what if I'm only 23?

So? Do you think that being young means that you can't die? You still need a plan. For instance, if you're 23 and unmarried, and you die, your assets may go to your parents, which might not make any sense. Leaving money to a sibling is considered more practical because, in estate planning, the flow of money generally tends to be downward, passing to younger generations. If you die at 23 and leave considerable assets to your parents, your property will first be taxed in your estate and then, when they die, in theirs (assuming they pass the money along to their surviving children). Why add that extra level of taxation? (Unless, of course, you hate your siblings.)

And if you're young and have children, you absolutely need an estate plan, because you must designate a guardian (although the court can turn down the request if it feels your choice isn't in the children's best interest). Otherwise, the courts go to the law of the state you lived in to determine who has priority to act as a guardian. This situation may be dreadful—do you really want your kids to live with Aunt Cruella?

4. Can't my husband/partner take care of it?

Being married—if that's what you happen to be—doesn't change any of this.

We live in a patriarchal society, and that means that sometimes men can intimidate and control us. And many women have difficulty asserting their own interest when it comes to estate planning, even in community-property states such as California, where the wife owns half of everything the husband earns (and vice-versa). Some women feel that their husband will resent them if they speak up about their wills. One friend of mine and her husband went to their lawyer to plan their estate, and while in session, they agreed perfectly on how to divide their assets. The next day, she called the lawyer back to tell him what she really wanted. She'd been afraid to say it in front of her husband.

Like everything else, if you're married, share your estate planning. You probably won't agree on everything, but try to work out reasonable compromises that make you both happy.

5. When should I initiate and revisit my plan?

Pay attention to estate planning as soon as you have assets. And don't let your concern lapse. This doesn't mean that you should see an estate planner every year, but what about after you've had a new child? Or your father has died? Or you've won the lottery?

Without doubt our culture prefers avoiding the subject of death. It makes us uncomfortable. But preparing a plan doesn't mean you're going to die now. It just means you understand reality and that you want your assets to be sensibly distributed.

Once it's in place, you should revisit your plan every few years or so. Life's circumstances change regularly, and so do finances. And the laws change, too.

Furthermore, try to coordinate your estate planning with the other aspects of your financial planning. What you do today regarding your investments and income-tax planning is part of a long-term strategy for providing for your family that doesn't conclude at your death.

And when you read the rest of these questions, keep in mind that estate planning is a complicated, ever-changing field. What you read here today may not be true tomorrow.

6. What are my assets and what is their value?

Understanding all your assets is a good start to establishing your estate plan, along with the knowledge of which are taxable and which aren't.

Your basic assets include: real estate; stocks, bonds, mutual-fund shares, and cash; tangible personal property, such as furniture, cars, jewelry; business or investment partnership interests; jointly owned property in any of the above categories; life insurance; retirement plans.

The laws vary concerning joint ownership with a spouse and/or with others, although generally, if you jointly own property with a spouse, one-half of the value is included as an asset of the estate. If you jointly own property with another person, 100 percent of the property will be included in your estate, unless you can prove that the joint owner contributed some or all of the consideration for the property.

Increasingly, pension plans are most people's largest asset, because they grow tax-free for years, along with your regular additions of principal. However, the real value of these assets is less than it seems, because these plans are subject to income tax when you withdraw money; they are subject to estate taxes; and they may be subject to an excise tax, for excess amounts withdrawn each year, or an **excess accumulation** tax after death, which means that you've accumulated too much (the rules seem to change yearly, so be sure to check them thoroughly).

THE SINGLE MOST IMPORTANT FIGURE TO KNOW: An estate with assets under $600,000 (increasing annually to $1,000,000 in the year 2006) is, with a few exceptions, not subject to federal death taxes.

Also keep in mind that, although you may be well under that lifetime exemption amount now, by the time you die, your assets may have accumulated enough interest to have grown past that mark. (If nothing else, your life insurance may instantaneously balloon your total asset value above the lifetime exemption amount.) So when you plan, factor in the future value of your assets as well as the present value. You don't want your estate to be overtaxed just because you didn't plan on being taxed at all.

Some states don't have a similar cutoff, and impose their own tax at other levels. Check and see if your state is one of them.

By the way, if you have an estate of $800,000, they don't simply deduct $600,000 and tax the last $200,000. They tax the entire $800,000, and then subtract $600,000 worth, or what comes to $192,800. So when they say everyone gets that $600,000 exemption, what they really mean is everyone gets a $192,800 tax credit (increasing to $345,800 in 2006).

Why is it that they never say what they really mean?

And the rate is graded. Unfortunately, it's quite complicated. It starts at 18 percent and goes up to 55 percent. So let's say you had an estate of $750,000. You would be taxed at an effective rate of approximately 33 percent, meaning you would owe $248,300. Then you would deduct that $192,800, which takes care of the first $600,000. And your estate would pay $55,500.

Is that perfectly clear?

7. What about my spouse?

If you're married, you can leave your spouse as much as you want without paying taxes. This is called the **marital deduction,** and it's extremely important. Much of estate planning involves the countless methods the ever-imaginative legal profession has invented to allow people to transfer property to spouses to avoid or delay estate taxes.

Thus a surviving spouse doesn't have to pay estate taxes until she dies. (Unless—why is there always an unless?—your surviving spouse isn't a U.S. citizen. Then you need to give your property to a trust held in the United States. If your husband Nigel moves back to London after your death, the IRS wants your assets to remain here.)

This doesn't mean, however, that you should simply leave everything to your spouse and forget about it. If you overfund your spouse's estate, his post-death taxes may be enormous, and the rest of your heirs will suffer. In other words, you can find ways to pass money along to your heirs without leaving it all to your spouse, even though he won't be taxed on it today.

The best way to do this is to give money now rather than later.

8. Why is a lifetime of giving away money so smart?

Knowing how to give well is a rare talent. And without knowledge of how estate taxes work, you won't give tax-intelligently.

The American system of death taxes and gift taxes is a unified system—in other words, the two have identical taxes and rates. A lifetime gift of $10,000 has the same structure as one bequeathed in a will.

From a tax viewpoint, there are four kinds of gifts:

1) *Untaxable cash gifts.* Throughout your life, you're allowed to give up to $10,000 annually to an unlimited number of recipients or, if you're married and your spouse consents to the gift, together you can give $20,000.

REMEMBER THIS FIGURE: $10,000. It's the other important number you need to know. (By the way, this means that if you and your husband throw your daughter a huge $50,000 wedding, you've given her, besides an affair she'll always remember, a taxable gift.)

2) *Ed/med gifts.* These are educational and medical gifts paid directly to an institution rather than to an individual.

Perhaps your father says to you, "Considering my doctor's bill, I can't pay my rent this month—can you give me the money to pay for it?" If that bill is for more than $10,000, you're taxed on what you give your dad. But if you pay the doctor bill directly, the gift won't be taxed, because the payment of medical bills is not subject to a gift tax.

Similarly, if you give a child $20,000 to pay for tuition, you'll be taxed on it. But if you pay the educational costs directly to the school, you won't.

3) *Gifts that use up your lifetime gift and estate tax exemption.* Let's say you give your daughter $50,000. The first $10,000 of that is excluded from tax consideration. Now, you don't have to pay taxes on that other $40,000 today. But you have lost $40,000 of your lifetime exemption, meaning that it's now down to $560,000. In other words, the IRS watches you for life. Just because you gave a gift twenty years ago doesn't mean that they won't remember. They're like elephants, without the charm.

4) *Gifts that incur gift tax.* These are gifts you bestow after you've used up all your tax exemptions; now you owe tax on everything you give.

If you have an estate that's going to be subject to federal taxes (i.e., your estate is bigger than the lifetime exemption amount)—and your attitude toward your heirs is good—you might want to consider some kind of gift-giving program to offset the tax bill.

For example, if you have a million-dollar estate, and over the last 25 years you've been giving your daughter Lily $10,000 a year, she already has $250,000 of your estate, tax-free. Furthermore, you've taken $250,000 out of your estate, which means it won't be taxed there, either. So you have $750,000 left. The $750,000 is then taxed at an effective rate of approximately 33 percent, which, after that $192,800 credit we all get, means a tax of $55,500. So Lily receives $694,500, plus the $250,000 she already has, for a total of $944,500.

But if you died and left Lily the entire million, your tax would come to $345,800, minus that $600,000 credit—which is always $192,800. That leaves $153,000 to taxes, and gives your daughter only $847,000.

The first way, you've saved $97,500 on taxes.

When thinking of giving gifts to grandchildren and later generations,

watch out for something called a **generation-skipping transfer tax.**
The idea here is to make sure that the government gets its fair share
—or what it thinks is its fair share—by trying to rake in the taxes it
would have made if the money had been left to the adult child who
then left it to the grandchild. (Still with me?) However, the first
million dollars in gifts to grandchildren and other "skip" people is
exempt from this tax—so a grandmother and grandfather can give $2
million in generation-skipping transfers. After this amount, gifts and
bequests are taxed at a rate of 55 percent on top of any estate or gift
tax otherwise due.

There's another huge advantage to giving a gift during someone's
lifetime: You can hear the person say, "Thank you." Also, you can
see her use the money, and take genuine pleasure in the resulting
improvement in her life-style. At its heart, I do hope giving will always
be about something more than saving tax money.

9. Why do I need to know about trusts?

There are many kinds of trusts, but basically they can be divided
into two groups: **revocable** and **irrevocable.** Revocable trusts can be
used as substitutes for wills and are used primarily to minimize the
probate period. These have no tax benefits.

Irrevocable trusts are exactly that: irreversible. They're designed to
dictate the conditions of your estate and to avoid taxes (legally). You
want to be pretty sure of yourself when you create one. You can't
un-create it.

There are many kinds of irrevocable trusts, and your estate planner
can tell you which, if any, are best for you. Usually, they're only for
those with estates worth more than the lifetime exemption amount.

But as long as you asked—you did ask, didn't you?—here's a run-
down of just a few.

• *QTIP.* (Yes, a QTIP—a qualified terminable interest property
trust.) A QTIP is what's known as a marital-deduction trust for a
surviving spouse.

Let's say you're married to your second husband (whom you love),
and have children from the first marriage (whom you also love), and
you want them to receive some of your estate, but you also want to

provide for your surviving spouse during his lifetime. If you leave the money outright to your spouse, you have no guarantee that he'll eventually leave that money to your children. If you leave the money to your children, there's no guarantee that they'll help out the surviving spouse.

However, if you leave your estate in a QTIP trust, you're entitled to a full marital deduction for the property passing to the trust, and no estate taxes on the property will be due until the death of your spouse. (You can't avoid the tax altogether, but you can delay it.) So what you've essentially done is given your spouse a guaranteed income for life, and then made sure that the money goes to your kids after he dies.

Naturally, certain restrictions apply.

• *CRT* (charitable remainder trust). Here you name a charitable organization that will eventually receive an asset. In the meantime you, your spouse, or anyone you choose receives income from that asset in the trust. Then, when you die, the asset goes to the charity. This makes sense particularly for those who are charitably inclined and don't need the principal of the trust for their personal expenses. And, you receive a substantial income-tax deduction for your charitable donation based on the property the charity will eventually receive. Plus, the property is taken out of your estate, reducing your estate taxes.

• *GRIT* (grantor retained income trust). Here you put your house into a trust for ten years, and give yourself the right to use it for those ten years. Let's say the house is worth a million dollars. Go to a set of actuarial tables to see how much it's worth to you to use the house for those ten years. Let's say it's worth $400,000. That means you've retained $400,000 worth of house, and so you've gifted $600,000. So here you've transferred a million-dollar asset for the price of a $600,000 gift, and you've retained the house for ten years, too. (Unless you die in the ninth year, and then all bets are off.)

If you live longer than ten years and still want to stay in the house, then you can rent it from the kids—provided they let you. Kids! But if all works out as planned, and you die after the ten years, you've transferred your million-dollar home for $600,000. And on top of that, if the house has appreciated to $2 million over those ten years, then you've transferred a $2 million house for $600,000. Congratulations! You've won a tax game.

And there are so many more—bypasses, GRATs (grantor retained annuity trusts), charitable lead trusts, and others. However, I can just see the eyeballs rolling in your head. Yes, it would be much easier if we didn't have to die and cause all this trouble. But you can save your heirs a lot of money by talking to someone who's spent her life studying these things.

10. And what's the other kind of trust?

A revocable trust, also called a **living trust,** or an *inter vivos* trust, is set up while you're alive. In it you place all your assets, including your money, your house, even your furniture. Your trustee then pays your bills and invests your money.

By doing this, you've arranged it so your estate is no longer subject to probate administration, and so your estate's trustee can take immediate charge of it. For many people, avoiding **probate** can be cost-effective, as well as timely. (Probate means the process of proving to the appropriate court that your will is genuine, so it can be administered according to your specifications.)

Without a living trust, generally no one can access your property to pay your bills after your death until your will is admitted to probate and an executor is named. This kind of trust doesn't save estate taxes, however.

If you become incapacitated and unable to manage your money, the court may have to appoint a guardian to take care of these duties. This is an expensive and intrusive proceeding. A living trust avoids this, as you have already named a person to act as trustee if you are no longer able to do so. You can also sign a **durable power of attorney** (see below).

Essentially, all trusts allow you to control your property after your death: You decide, within limits, who receives how much and when they receive it. If you want your spouse to think twice before remarrying after your death, you might provide that his rights to receive money from the trust cease upon his remarriage. But don't go crazy. Courts don't like wacky provisions. For instance, no matter how much you dislike your daughter-in-law Esmerelda, courts shy away from provisions that require your son to slap Esmerelda in public before he can receive benefits from the trust. Encouraging abuse is against public policy. It's bad enough while you're alive, but don't try to control others from the grave.

11. Is life insurance taxable?

If you own a life-insurance policy, the proceeds of the policy aren't counted as income or taxable to the beneficiary of the policy.

However, the proceeds *are* included in your estate for estate-tax purposes.

Let's say you've got $600,000 in cash assets and a life-insurance policy that will pay $200,000 at your death. Your gross estate, for tax purposes, is $800,000. The beneficiary of your $200,000 policy won't have to report the $200,000 on her income tax. But your executor *will* have to include it as part of your gross estate for tax purposes. Thus, owning life insurance doesn't reduce your estate taxes and, in fact, can increase them.

If, however, you already own life insurance or are planning to purchase it, you can save these taxes by transferring ownership of the policy to an insurance trust.

An insurance trust is for those whose estate exceeds the lifetime exemption amount cutoff, and it is one of the biggest tax-saving devices available. Its motive is to take, say, a million dollars out of the death-tax picture. Otherwise, you might find yourself paying off $500,000 in taxes generated by the insurance value.

It's quite simple. For instance, an independent trustee buys the insurance, and you fund the trust to pay the premiums. It costs you only the attorney fee. The down side is that you no longer "own" the policy—i.e., you can't borrow against it, you can't change the beneficiaries, you can't do a thing.

But here's something else: If you own a million dollars' worth of insurance, and the premium is $10,000 a year, you'll want to give the trustee that $10,000 without gift tax consequences.

Remember: If you give $10,000 a year as a gift, that money isn't taxed.

Here's where something called a **Crummey trust** comes in (yes, Virginia, there really were Crummeys. They lived in California and just happened to have a terrible name to lend to the law). The Crummey trust allows you to give that $10,000 to a trust tax-free—the purpose of a Crummey is always to transfer property in a manner so that the gift qualifies for that annual exclusion from the gift tax we've been talking about.

To initiate the Crummey trust in this instance, when the trustee gets that money, he must send a letter to, for instance, your son the beneficiary, saying that he, the trustee, just received that $10,000 from you, and that your son has the right for thirty days to demand that money. Of course, your son isn't really going to ask for it, but by giving him the right to a present interest, the exclusion is activated. So you can treat that $10,000 as free of gift tax.

(Crummey trusts are very valuable tools, and can work for all kinds of assets: stock, real estate, etc. There's much more to them than we need to go into here. If you're interested in these trusts, you could easily quit your job, take a year off from your life, go to a desert island, and study them. By the time you return, however, the laws will probably have changed again. Anyway, I'm sure you can find something more interesting to do.)

12. How can I tell how much I can afford to transfer or give away during my lifetime?

If you're working for a living—as most of us are—you may already be financially stretched. Yes, saving taxes legally is a great thing, but don't give away all your money to save taxes! Focus on what you realistically need for the last years of your life, and leave yourself room to enjoy yourself.

Planning involves the future and the present—by carefully analyzing what you can afford to give away today, it may force you to think about ten, or twenty, or thirty years from now, giving you some clarity about your financial needs and goals.

Always make sure that you've left some money liquid after your death, because your family may need cash to pay for funeral costs, legal fees, taxes, and so on. Imagine if for some reason your estate takes time to settle, and in the meantime those you love have to borrow money to take care of your last needs.

13. Who should advise me regarding my plan?

Lawyers have traditionally given estate-planning advice, and up until a few decades ago that consultation wasn't very complicated. But the era of specialization in all things has arrived, and that includes estate planning. Today, in many states, lawyers receive bar certification as specialists in estate and trust planning, the same way a lawyer might specialize in tax law or workers' compensation.

Certified Financial Planners also work in this area. Still, the CFP will need to consult with a qualified lawyer, and so it might be practical simply to work with one person.

14. How much does a will cost?

Drawing up a will costs less than setting up a trust, but the amount varies. You can probably spend anywhere from $300 to $3,000. If it's done right, you save much more than that in the long run.

Estate planning can cost anything from a few hundred dollars to a few thousand. Again, it depends on whom you see, what you need, and how complicated your picture is.

15. Where do I keep my will?

If your lawyer maintains space in the office for wills, that's probably the best place. Many law firms rent vaults at banks or have separate safe storage areas for important documents. If your lawyer doesn't maintain such space, you should keep the will in a secure, fireproof place in your home. It isn't a good idea to keep it in a safe-deposit box, because once you die, the laws in many states make it difficult for anyone to open the box until someone is appointed executor of your estate (which cannot be done until the will is offered for probate). So if you insist on keeping it in a box, think about giving someone else access.

16. Do I absolutely have to go to a lawyer about my will?

If your estate is simple, and your bequests minimal, some states allow you to create a **holographic will.** This means that it's handwritten. Sign it, date it, and, if the state requires, have it witnessed; then store it with your important papers, and it becomes your will.

In any state, if your estate is small, you don't have minor children, and you want your property to pass as it would under the laws of intestacy, you may not need a will at all.

17. What is a power of attorney?

Generally, a power of attorney pertains to financial matters (and/or health—see number 18). A financial power of attorney allows the person you select to do your banking, real-estate transactions, insurance purchases, etc. This person, who becomes your attorney-in-fact, can take over today or at a future date.

Power of attorney is a fairly simple and cheap document to prepare, and is useful in a variety of circumstances. For instance, if you're planning a trip around the world and need someone to take care of your business, you can select an attorney-in-fact, and limit her powers to the time you're gone.

If you're elderly, it's a good idea to name a trusted friend or relative as attorney-in-fact now. Then, if you become disabled or incompetent, the attorney-in-fact can write checks on your behalf, deposit Social Security checks, etc., without requiring the court's interference.

18. Is a living will a financial document?

No. A living will explains your preferences regarding life-sustaining treatment and related medical procedures.

If you've been in an accident, you may not wish to be kept alive with life-prolonging medical intervention. A living will lets your relatives know your medical preferences.

Many states also authorize you to designate a health-care agent using a power of attorney; this person will be able to make medical decisions for you if you're unable to express your wishes.

19. What's a letter of instruction?

A letter of instruction tells your survivors everything they need to know right after you've died. You don't need a lawyer to write one, for its purpose is more practical than legal. The idea is to let everyone know what you want to happen, and why. You might include instructions on whom to contact, or you might want to let your survivors know the details of your estate: assets, debts, the location of personal papers. And, of course, if you have any special wishes, this is a good place to let them be known. For those of you who feel you're worth it, you can write your own obituary for publication. But this isn't the time to mention that you want Cousin Bertha to get the Rolls-Royce. She's not legally bound to inherit it through this letter.

20. Who should I pick to be my executors/trustees?

Please, carefully consider the person you wish to name as executor of your will.

A lot of psychology goes into planning your estate. You want to consider all the people involved—their present responsibilities, marriages, intrinsic character. Perhaps your son Cain is the apple of your eye, but he's been locked in a drug-rehabilitation center for three years, and besides, he's sworn off speaking English because it's the language of capitalist oppressors. Is he really a good choice to be your executor—no matter how much you love him?

And don't worry about offending someone. For example, even if you know Cain would be hurt if he found out that you picked second son Joseph instead, this isn't the time for sibling rivalries to color your choice. Take Joseph, a capable lawyer and steady man, and leave Cain enough money to make him happy.

I know of one couple who paid top dollar for a good estate lawyer, but they never finished their plan because they couldn't agree on whom to pick as executor. Now the couple is divorced, so they both need new plans anyway.

21. Is dying tax-deductible?

Some parts of it are. For instance, funeral expenses, attorney's fees, the administration of the estate, debts, and unpaid mortgages are among the morbid deductions the government allows on your estate-tax return. Also, if you live in a state where estates are taxed, that tax may be deductible, too. Have your lawyer/tax adviser look into this for you, since the time following the death of a relative or a close friend may not be the time you're thinking most clearly of hanging on to all those receipts.

But please: Don't die just for the tax benefits.

Chapter 7

Choosing Life, and Insuring It Well

You don't need to pray to God anymore when there are storms in
the sky, but you do have to be insured.

Ambrose Bierce

*I*n the movie version of *The Wizard of Oz,* after the Wicked Witch
of the West's winged monkeys have pulled the stuffing out of the
Scarecrow, he's lying down, exhausted, his straw littering the ground
around him, barely enough left inside to carry on. ("That's you all
over," the Tin Woodman tells him.) I never empathized with a scarecrow more, except that he seemed to have more insides remaining
than I had.

Scared, sleepless, and empty, I couldn't eat, sleep, or think. My
weight had dropped to eighty pounds. I felt like a wreck after a wreck
after a wreck, like a car that had been in an accident, and then, as it
was being towed away, had been plowed into again. And again. These
were my fathers' friends. He had trusted them. How could they do
this to his helpless daughter?

They looked for any means of intimidation. But I had two things in
my favor, and both were powerful. One was Dr. Call, who said, "Grow
up. Good guys don't win. Bad guys don't get punished. You have to
fight." He shook me into reality.

And then there was Allen, who presented me with a check for
$35,000. "Put it in the bank and live off of it," he said. "Pay me back
when we beat these guys." Otherwise I had nowhere to go. I had no
savings and no resources. I was at rock bottom.

But reality doesn't care if you're in a bad mood.

They deposed me. We deposed them. We subpoenaed their wives. The world was one grand deposition. "How can we do this to their wives?" I asked Allen. "Women shouldn't be involved in this."

"You're a woman," he said. "Look what they're doing to you. Aren't they trying to take the gold right out of your teeth?"

I was startled: The idea that women should become a part of this! I had forgotten that they'd already done it to me.

The war raged for several weeks until Allen was finally able to badger them into a reasonable compromise.

I also received $50,000 from a wrongful-death claim with the airline on whose flight my mother and sister had been killed.

Not knowing what else to do with all this money, I paid Allen back and bought a CD with the $100,000 I now had to invest. Interest rates were 17 percent then—which, they told me, was an extraordinarily high rate, and so I was earning $17,000. That, along with the rental income of $18,000, meant $35,000 a year, or $25,000 a year less than I was used to.

And of course, when I bought the CD from the bank, I walked away with the banker, whom I was now dating. He wasn't Allen, but I needed a man in my life. I wasn't ready to consider the alternative. And I was still grieving for my family, and trying to decide how to survive financially in the long term. The money wasn't going to last.

Anxiety over these worries drove me to my greatest solace—outside of my children and my man of the moment—which was my garden, the sole reason I had bought my house. Its facade resembled that of any other modern Californian home, but once inside, past large glass walls, you could look out on beautiful gardens where I had planted dozens of brilliant flowers and bulbs. The garden grounded me, the activity was meditative; the flowers, so constantly beautiful, lent my life stability.

When I moved in, the yard was surrounded by a good deal of gravel, and my primary project was to remove it all so that the plants could bloom anywhere and everywhere. One warm, fall afternoon I was digging up rocks and replacing them with dirt when I felt a sudden twinge in my arm. I didn't give it much attention at the time, but by the middle of the night the pain was excruciating.

The only course of action I could think of was to get to the local emergency room, which I did; there the doctor decided it was just a muscle spasm, so he gave me a bottle of relaxants and told me to go home and sleep.

But by the next day the pain had grown considerably. This time I called my own doctor who, after examining me, was baffled. But when the pain only increased, he sent me back to the hospital, where they immediately put me into traction, turning me into the proverbial human dartboard, taking test after test with needle after needle. And still they couldn't figure out the problem.

Finally they brought in Two Very Serious Doctors, an orthopedist and a neurosurgeon. They, too, were mystified, which was even more frightening. Everyone's dead, I thought, the partners have taken my financial security, my body is unidentifiably sick, my kids are terrified, and these men in suits don't have a clue.

I needed an operation, the doctors said, and there was a chance I might become paralyzed for life, although they couldn't explain why. I seldom understood what these doctors were saying; much of it sounded like gibberish, but in addition my mind, body, and spirit, as well as my hearing, were numb with the Demerol the staff was feeding me. There had been a time when I had enjoyed dulling my mind; now those same feelings scared me.

Around this time the gynecologist popped in to say a cheery hello and, by the way, she added, she'd found a tumor on my remaining ovary and I had to have a hysterectomy as soon as I recovered from the other operation.

I remember sitting in a wheelchair on the morning of my birthday, waiting for an X ray, and sobbing hysterically. They were taking out my uterus, my ovaries, and as far as I knew, they were taking my arm, too. I had lost my family, most of my income, and now they were carting away body parts.

But fate is a strange operator. I can relate the events as they occurred next, but I can't explain them. In that cold, dismal waiting room, something remarkable took place inside my psyche. One minute I was drenched in despair; the next minute, I was transcendent. I looked inside myself and for the first time in my life, I saw real strength. I had shed my fear. I knew I could live without my left arm, my ovaries, and anything else they took out. The key word was *live*. As long as I was alive, I knew I'd always have my kids, and they would have me. I could learn to live my life as well as before. I could use my right arm as I had once used the left one. I could do anything.

That extraordinary transformation from resignation to confidence had taken place without my knowledge or understanding, without even my conscious awareness. Perhaps it was the result of all I had been through, perhaps it was due to my therapy, perhaps I'll never know. Frankly, I don't ever need to. Because there it was: courage, now as much a part of my personality as fear had been before.

A few minutes later the X-ray technician wheeled me into the operating room. Once there I looked the doctor straight in the eye and said, "If you kill me, you're leaving two orphans on this earth. My daughters have no one else." I fully intended to be alive when I woke up, even if I didn't have an arm or a voice.

The operation went ahead, and in the end, I profited from some real luck. The problem turned out to be a herniated disk in my neck, and after they performed the operation to remove the disk, as well as the hysterectomy, my body normalized.

After six weeks of hospitalization, on New Year's Day 1981, they even let me go home. Once there I promised my kids—God knows how I could do this, but it turned out to be a promise kept—that we would never be forced apart from one another again.

I was also lucky because, just six weeks before, a friend, horrified that I didn't have health insurance, induced me to join his group plan. If he hadn't, I'd have been faced with bankruptcy once again.

◆ ◆ ◆

That first night back home, a nurse was supposed to stay with me, but when she failed to appear, some of my old fear showed up instead and I couldn't sleep. At midnight I received an obscene phone call, but while the man was breathing his filth at me, my resilience returned in spades. "How *dare* you do this to me," I erupted. "I just got out of the hospital and my kids are scared to death and I'm lying here in a neck brace."

"I'm so sorry," the poor, sick man wailed. "If I had known, I'd never have called. I'll try someone else."

The next day the X-ray technician from the hospital called to ask if he could drop by for a few hours to see how I was doing. He ended up staying for a year, to no one's great surprise.

My therapy hadn't stopped during my hospital stay. I had already dealt with my first major issue: the grief. The next issue was figuring out how to take care of myself, which I was learning. I was also accepting the fact that, from now on, I would have to fend for myself, and that I, and no one else, was responsible for creating my family's financial security.

And, as I'd discovered at the hospital, I did have strength. I'd faced all those issues: cancer, the marriage and divorce, drugs, my father's death, the plane crash, the fight for my money, the illnesses, and I'd gotten through each one. I'd learned that tragedy can destroy you, or it can become your best weapon. For if you can live through these traumas, you can stand up and face anything. And that's what I decided to do: stand up.

Among the many things I now did was make sure that I was properly insured. When my father died without insurance, the rest of us suffered. I wanted to guarantee that my kids would never have to. My father had left us job-related policies worth about $60,000, but he could have given us ten times that amount without a significant investment. He didn't have the cash, due to his gambling debts. That $60,000 couldn't come close to compensating for the huge income he'd been making, and which we'd grown used to having.

My mother could easily have insured herself, but she didn't live long enough after my father's death to learn about money, much less insurance. Regardless, my mother didn't see herself as protection for me; she looked to me for protection.

Insurance

So what is insurance anyway? Protection is exactly the right word: Insurance protects you against loss. Before you start to grow your money, you have to make sure you guard what you have, or you may not have it. What could be simpler?

Start with an automobile. Let's say a new car costs $20,000. How many single purchases in your lifetime will be more expensive than that? Unless you're very rich and in the habit of buying diamonds and minks, the odds are good that after your home, your car is your single biggest acquisition.

Now, think of all the maniacs out on the roads. If one of them happens to broadside you while he's talking on his car phone, slurping his coffee, and running a red light, you could be in real trouble. What if the maniac doesn't stop and you don't get his license-plate number? What if he's not insured and can't afford to pay for your repairs? You have to be prepared for these possibilities.

Think of all the other maniacs who want to steal your car. If one morning you wake up and that car is gone, you're going to need a new one pretty soon. So what's $1,500 a year to make sure that you protect your $20,000? That's what insurance is. You sleep better at night knowing that, by paying out a small amount of money, you're guaranteeing that you don't lose a huge amount.

◆ ◆ ◆

As with any other kind of planning, one of the first items on your insurance agenda is the person with whom you will work. You want a good insurance agent to possess the same qualities as any other professional: honesty, dependability, intelligence.

How do you know if your agent is good? First, make sure she's referred by someone you know and trust. Then, trust your own instincts. How does she talk? Does she appear to be a good listener? She may not be brilliant, but if she's got good antennae, she'll know how to ask you the right questions to extract a sense of your particular needs, and she won't make any recommendations until she feels that she knows you well. One familiar insurance agents' maxim goes: "People don't buy our products because they understand them. They buy our products because they feel we understand them."

And it doesn't hurt to find someone with a good deal of experience and the proper degrees. Ask for references, too. Does she know someone else who does what you do for a living? For instance, if you're an artist, the fact that she's working with other artists might mean that she's already searched out good programs for your needs.

◆ ◆ ◆

Following are the types of insurance to consider:

- *Health insurance:* to ensure that you won't suffer a financial loss if your health is impaired.
- *Homeowner's insurance:* to insure your property against theft or destruction. If you rent, renter's insurance protects your personal property similarly.
- *Automobile insurance:* to cover your own liability if you hurt someone else, to cover your own medical and automobile costs if you're hurt or your car is damaged in an accident, and for financial protection against an incident involving someone who's uninsured.
- *Personal liability insurance:* to protect your personal assets from a personal liability lawsuit.
- *Professional liability insurance:* to protect your professional assets from a job-related lawsuit.
- *Disability insurance:* to replace as much of your income as possible in case of a long-term disability.
- *Life insurance:* to replace your wage income in the event of your death, as well as to use for estate taxes, if you have assets, and possibly for investment purposes.

Except for life insurance, which is not essential for everyone, the others are necessary. I mean it. You can't consider yourself financially sound if you're not insured. You could be hit by a car and rack up a $50,000 hospital bill in no time, or come down with an illness so severe you can't work anymore and, presto, there goes your nice salary and whatever savings you've accumulated.

In fact, **health insurance** is the most important purchase a woman can make if she is or becomes single and isn't insured through her workplace. A bad illness can simply knock you out of the box. And then what happens? You end up a ward of the state, at the mercy of the county. You no longer have a choice of doctor or treatment. Whenever I hear people say, "I can't afford medical insurance," I say, "No, no, you can't afford not to have it."

If full coverage is too expensive, then at least get catastrophic (hospitalization) insurance. This type of coverage means that you're not insured for doctors' visits, but you are covered if, by some misfortune, you end up in the hospital.

Many of the women I see tell me that they don't need to know anything about health insurance because they're covered through their husband's employer-sponsored health plan. And often they're right. But it isn't enough to know coverage exists, since it varies widely. Examine it. Make sure the employer is giving you good benefits. If not, you can either lobby for change, or decide that you need an extra layer of protection, which is fairly inexpensive and can save you a bushel in the long run.

And if your program's coverage seems unfair, don't passively accept a claim rejection. Argue! Contest the claim! You can win. Insurance companies always prefer not to pay. When you know you're right, don't surrender without a fight.

How much health insurance do you actually need? Sometimes it's a matter of how much you can afford rather than how much you need. If I were on my own, I'd want the best protection possible, but good individual coverage is expensive. So, given both the rising price of surgery and the fact that I might not be able to afford an annual $9,000 health insurance bill, I'd need to establish limits.

First, I'd start by telling my agent that my budget isn't an issue. Then, after she informed me of all the options, I'd say to her, "Okay,

Ms. Agent, if you were me and you *did* have a budget, what would you now eliminate?" If she's good, she'll go back over the options and create a plan best suited for you.

There are many, many areas to consider; here are only a few of the more important ones.

Coverage limits are a cost limit per illness, or per surgical procedure. Back in the 1980s, surgeons were able to charge almost anything they wanted for an operation because, since there were no insurance limits, patients didn't care how much a procedure cost. Now, insurance carriers decide what each surgical procedure is worth, and then place a limit on it in the policy. If you want the best surgeon in your city, and she charges $35,000, and your policy has a $6,000 limit, you've got a problem. So always be clear on your policy's individual surgical limits.

You also want to check out overall limits. Your policy may state that the coverage won't climb past $50,000, or $100,000, in medical expenses. Obviously, you want that limit to be as high as possible.

Co-insurance and deductibles are also important. Co-insurance means that you must pay, perhaps, 20 percent of all your health costs. In the long run, that will keep the cost of your insurance down. And, as a financial participant, you'll pay attention to what you're being charged, because you're paying 20 percent of it.

As for deductibles: If yours is $3,000, that means that you pay the first $3,000 of medical costs, and after that the insurance kicks in at whatever percentage your policy stipulates. Again, this helps control the cost of your policy, since the insurance company doesn't have to fool with your small claims, such as the flu, allergies, etc.

Outside of insurance, of course, are the ubiquitous **HMOs**—or health maintenance organizations. Here you join an organization, pay monthly fees, and receive primary medical care from a single health provider. No insurance is involved. What you get is lower payments, and what you lose is flexibility in choosing a doctor. Another option is a **PPO,** or preferred provider organization, which consists of doctors who, by working together, can offer health services at cheaper rates to members. A PPO gives you more freedom to pick your doctor. Still another option is an **EPO,** or exclusive provider organization, which tends to be cheaper and offers a smaller network of doctors. Unlike a PPO, in which you can always choose to disregard the membership roll of doctors and go off on your own, an EPO is exclusive.

Whatever you choose, please consider your health insurance as carefully as you guard your health. Suffering through a debilitating illness is difficult enough—why make it worse by worrying about whether you can afford proper care?

As always, be honest when filling out your forms. Don't leave out any prior conditions and don't lie about claims. Honesty is an end in itself, but practically speaking, if anyone ever discovers that you've lied on your forms, you could lose your policy and your benefits. It isn't worth it.

◆ ◆ ◆

Something else to consider is **long-term care** insurance, which helps you look after yourself in the event of a prolonged illness or disability. Women often think that Medicare will cover all their nursing-home expenses, but unfortunately, that's not so.

Also unfortunately, long-term care can be expensive. Premiums for a woman in her mid-60s may cost more than $4,000 a year, depending on the policy. Still, this insurance is extremely valuable, particularly for those who fear that their long-term care costs will devour their estate, leaving their children without assets. The average cost of a year's stay at a nursing home now exceeds $25,000, and in twenty years that figure could easily double.

I find that women usually have more need of long-term care than their male spouses because, statistically, men are more likely to become ill first. Typically a wife will take care of her husband when possible, but often, when she needs similar help, the male is either too ill to return that help, or has died. For better or worse, husbands don't turn into caretakers as often as wives do.

If you can afford it, your long-term policy should cover all kinds of nursing care rather than certain circumstances; it should last a lifetime rather than cover a limited period in a nursing home (after all, you probably won't want to leave the home when you reach 90), and it should cover all illnesses and conditions.

One tip: The younger you are when you buy it, the cheaper the policy will be. A policy that costs $500 a year when you're 45 could cost you many times that amount twenty years later.

◆ ◆ ◆

I can't say enough about **homeowner's insurance.** As you'll soon see, if I hadn't had it when my home burned down, I would have lost all my assets.

Homeowner's insurance is pretty simple. You get it to cover the property in your home (and in unattached structures such as a garage), and your liability if someone hurts herself on your property. It also covers the money you spend while living in a hotel if your house burns down. (If you rent, you should buy renter's insurance, for similar reasons.) Now you're covered in case of a theft, an accident, or most natural disasters.

In most states you can't close the deal on your home until you show evidence of fire insurance. So if the bank holding your mortgage thinks that it's that important, it probably should be important to you, too.

And consider **replacement-cost coverage,** which means that the assessed value of destroyed or lost items will be based on what it would cost you to buy new ones, rather than what the pieces themselves are worth. Replacement insurance costs more, but it's worth it. If your favorite ten-year-old sofa were ruined, its actual worth is low, but it might cost $1,500 to replace it.

Discounts and special deals are available; new homes can cost less to insure, security devices and smoke alarms bring savings, as can being over age 55. Look for any and all discounts you qualify for.

Other kinds of homeowner issues to consider are **floater policies,** which provide extra coverage for specific valuables, such as art and jewelry, and **safe-deposit coverage.** Believe it or not, your bank doesn't insure the possessions in your box, and if that's where you're storing Aunt Flossie's diamonds, you might want to make sure you're covered in case the bank is robbed. Aunt Flossie would kill you if anything happened to those jewels.

In order to ensure proper reimbursement, you should make a list of your possessions, and make a video (or take photos) of your valuable items. Note what things are worth, too, and be as specific as possible. And if you buv expensive new items, store the receipts and/or film them, too. Keep current!

◆ ◆ ◆

Auto insurance is fairly straightforward. Most states require that you purchase at least some. So if you have a car, and you obey the law, you may already have insurance.

But how do you know if your insurance is any good? You may well form a strong bond with the agent who works with you on your estate, on life insurance, or on disability insurance, but your auto insurance agent usually won't give you more than a short conference.

What can you do? Life insurance is complicated, but try reading an automobile policy.

Don't be afraid to tackle the subject seriously. Interview a few agents. Ask them how long they've been in the business, what companies they like, and why they do business with them. If you ask an agent why she recommends a certain product, and she won't give you a straight answer, that's bad. If she's a terrible listener, that's bad. Just asking the questions is more important than the answers. You get a chance to see how that person handles you.

Your auto agent should be able to sort through all your possibilities. Different states have different rules: Some require that you buy uninsured-motorist coverage, in case someone who's uninsured causes an accident. You always want bodily injury, property liability, and medical-payments insurance. But perhaps you don't need collision coverage, particularly if your car is old. And see if your health coverage duplicates your medical-payments auto coverage. Don't forget to look for discounts, too, available for those with good driving records, or a driver-training certificate, or who are old. (Who said there weren't any advantages to aging?)

Some companies sell you insurance directly, without having to use an agent. These companies can be very reputable, or not at all, so be careful before you sign on.

◆ ◆ ◆

Liability insurance is a misleading term because there are so many different types of liabilities, both personal and professional. For one business owner it may mean buying protection in case someone slips in her lobby and breaks a leg, while for another, it might mean buying protection against a wrongful-termination suit.

It's a very general term, therefore, and in this litigious age, a necessary item if you have any assets at all. Personal liability covers your nonwork life. Someone comes to your house, trips over a nail in your foyer, breaks her ankle, and says, "I can't ever sprint again, and that's what I do for a living." She then sues you for the income she would have made for the rest of her natural life. Liability insurance covers that suit. And it's not expensive.

Professional liability insurance is something all professionals should look into. If you're employed at a large firm, your company may provide it for you. Some professions are more liable than others—doctors, lawyers, accountants, architects, and nurses among them.

Since personal liability insurance doesn't protect you from business-related liability, you need both types—and one way to make sure you have enough coverage is with an **umbrella policy.** So many times I've mentioned umbrella policies to women only to have them look at me with complete bafflement. "Insure my umbrella?" someone once asked. (Really!)

Umbrella policies do exactly what they sound like they do: They extend your liability coverage in many areas, and this is something you may well need since the insurance field is prone to lots of fine print, and you don't want to lose your estate to some technicality. These policies are fairly cheap, perhaps $1,000 a year, and well worth the cost.

◆ ◆ ◆

Most women understand the concept of homeowner's insurance, because they're used to taking care of the home, and many understand health insurance because, as mothers, they know the costs and importance of maintaining family health.

What they seldom understand is disability. When you're dead, you don't need much. Dead is dead. But when you're sick, you still need warmth, food, clothing, and shelter. How will you live if you don't have any money coming in?

At this point in my life I understood the concept well. For now that I'd made the decision to lead my own life, I knew that no one was going to prop me up if I got hit by a car tomorrow. **Disability insurance** is so important for anyone dependent on a working income. Why don't more women get it? The other day I met with a single mother of two who'd been a vice president at an advertising agency until she came down with a debilitating nerve disorder that required three months of hospitalization, and then two additional years of in-home recuperation. Her excellent health insurance covered her hospital bills. But she hadn't given any thought to what would happen to her and her family without her income over those next few years. She ended up wiping out her savings account to cover her living expenses; now she's back at work, but terrified because her safety net has disappeared. And she was lucky—at least she had savings to use up.

If I were forced to buy only life or disability insurance, I'd pick disability. The chances of disability occurring are four times greater than death when you're young. If you put ten people in a room, at least two of them will have a long-term disability over the next ten to twenty years. Almost half of all people now 35 years old will be incapacitated for three months or longer before they're 65.

The problem is that disability has become such a hot item there aren't enough insurance carriers to cover the demand. In other words, buying disability is a little like sending your 16-year-old boy out to buy auto insurance. It's a sellers' market, unlike life insurance, which agents have to beg people to buy. Furthermore, it's gender-rated, which means that it's more expensive for women than men. Sad but true, and there's nothing anyone can do about this.

How much of this insurance should you have? It's very difficult to get disability in high amounts—the companies usually want to cap your limit at 50 to 60 percent of your present earnings. So buy as much as you can get or afford. And beware: It's not cheap.

(If you work at home, you'll have an even more difficult time getting disability insurance. Insurance companies seem to think there's some magic to showing up at an office every day. This area has been filled with fraudulent claims, and insurance companies feel that someone who goes to an office will have a harder time faking an injury than someone who stays home. And it's not that difficult to get a doctor to help you out, as doctors aren't always innocent when it comes to writing excuses. In fact, according to a friend of mine who studies the industry, over the last decade, as doctors' incomes have dropped, their own disability claims have risen substantially.)

There are several kinds of disability insurance. Some 95 percent of the market is made up of **guaranteed renewable non-cancelable,** which means that they can't take it away from you. You own it, you control it, and no one can change the premium. And that's the best kind to get.

Then there are budgeting issues. Maybe you can't afford $3,500 a year. Ask your agent to look for ways to reduce the premium. Perhaps you can get by on less than 50 percent of your income. Or maybe you're willing to go six months without requiring any benefits, which reduces the cost, too. Or you can limit the years of coverage. Perhaps you don't need benefits for a lifetime, but feel that twenty years is enough—although I'm not terribly fond of that strategy, because disabilities can be forever.

Regardless of how much you can afford, you can't afford not to have at least some disability insurance. With luck, you'll never file a claim. But it's nice to know it's there.

◆ ◆ ◆

Life insurance is a bit like the common cold: Nearly everyone gets it, but no one really seems to understand it. And for good reason— life insurance can be an essential part of any good financial portfolio, and it's also wildly complicated. The following explains only the barest fundamentals. Multivolume books have been written on this same subject, and they, too, apologize for not having enough room.

You don't have to read all of this if you don't wish, because if you have an agent whom you trust, she will explain your life insurance needs and whether, in fact, you need any life insurance at all. Not everyone does.

But before you skip over this section, do read at least the following:

All things considered, the type of life insurance product you choose should meet your needs and be affordable. Consider how much life insurance you truly require. If your spouse is your family's principal breadwinner, his insurance is more important than yours, and you and he should discuss whether you need it, too. You may not.

If you're single and no one's life will suffer from the loss of your income, your money would most likely do better elsewhere.

If you're a single mother, or the primary money-maker of the family, you probably do need life insurance. Perhaps the best way to find out is to estimate how much money your family lives on, and determine what would happen financially to the family if you were to die. You'd like your family to live well without you. As far as I'm concerned, that's the primary use of life insurance.

You may also have life insurance through your work—always check the benefits package when you take a job!

There are many other considerations with insurance, including various tax benefits and estate-planning benefits. There's no time to discuss those here, but make sure you ask your agent to tell you everything you ever need to know about this insurance.

In New York, Massachusetts, and Connecticut, you don't need an agent at all: Savings banks offer life insurance at low cost.

If using an agent is out of your budget, you can buy your insurance through direct-marketing companies. You won't get as much advice, however, so this option is best for those who know their way around insurance, or who have been counseled by someone knowledgeable and simply want to buy a particular product.

If you do use an agent, check her out carefully. If she's good, she'll work to combine your best interests with hers. If she's bad, she'll try to take you for the biggest commission she can. As a whole, life-insurance salesmen have a mixed reputation. Some want to sell you the moon. But you don't need the moon. You only need as much insurance as your own calculations indicate. Insurance rates vary widely. Shop around.

Check out the insurance company, too. Some companies have been poorly managed and were taken over by state regulators. You want to deal only with the highest-rated companies, for instance, those with Standard & Poor's AAA ratings. And keep abreast of changes in insurance—your insurance needs will change as you get older. Don't blindly stick with the same insurance program you've had for twenty years.

If you're truly interested in learning more about life insurance, read the appendix on page 189. But if you have an agent whom you trust, frankly, you may not need to. I probably wouldn't.

Chapter 8

Investing, and Becoming a Smart Investor

Money is like an arm or a leg—use it or lose it.

Henry Ford

*I*t was time to pay attention to my money before it withered away from neglect. I sought out the advice of an old friend, who recommended General Motors stock, which he considered both undervalued and a relatively safe investment.

I thought, The stock market? My father always thought that the market was too risky. "Buying a stock is just like making a bet," he used to say. Then I thought, My father? Really! I called a broker friend and bought 1,000 shares.

A day later GM was up one point, and that was that: I was hooked. I starting staring at the ticker tape like it was the world's most riveting soap opera. All I was doing was watching television, and in return my net worth was increasing. This was better than dialing for dollars.

The broker recommended we margin my account. "We just lend you half the money," he said. "You can buy twice as much stock."

"Fine," I said. What in the world were margins? "Do it!"

He did. The stock continued to rise.

"Now you've made four thousand dollars!" the broker said.

"This is great!" I said. "Now what?"

"Buy options!" he said. "Sell short!"

"Buy!" I said. "Sell!"

Well, that year I was long, I was short, I was into puts, I was into calls, and it never occurred to me to ask what the hell any of it meant.

This was some new kind of thrill-a-minute roller coaster. Maybe the gambler's instinct inherited from my father was kicking in. Or perhaps I was buoyed by how much playing stocks relieved my financial stress. Oh, I was making money!

Unfortunately, the broker loved this process too, so much so that he wasn't interested in keeping my investment safe. He just wanted to have fun. And it did look like fun, so much so that I began showing up at his office to watch the action. As a discount broker, the man's real job was to take orders, but instead he and his mother gambled with their clients' money as well as their own. That's right: his mother —an attractive, chain-smoking, coffee-guzzling elderly woman who sat in front of the ticker screaming her head off as if she was watching a wrestling match.

What goes up often comes down. The market took a downward spiral, and my money started to dwindle until we went on a real slide and, boom! there it was. No more money. Bye-bye $50,000. Back to square one—or square zero.

One day, while sitting on the beach and looking at the paperwork from my transactions, I noticed that, despite my losses, my broker had done quite well for himself. I made up my mind on the spot that I should become a broker, too. I was just as smart. If this man and his mother could make this kind of money, surely I could make at least a small income.

I was now living on interest from my cash and the one rental property I owned, and the total didn't add up to anything close to what I needed, so I sold my house and dipped into the principal every month, which even I knew was dangerous. I'd still never held a job outside of answering phones and working with my father. Of course, I was only 41 years old.

But I had made one important new ally: One of my closest friends was dating a very rich man who saw my interest in the market and, because he thought I was smart, and because he wanted to help, he offered me his account as a base. It was time for me to get a job, and this was my career choice. Learning how to invest money wisely soon became my main interest in life.

Investing

It's a fact, and one that I constantly have to confront in my business: Women are much more likely to fear investing than men. Now, there are, of course, exceptions. I took to it like a fish to water. But my life has always led me to odd places.

There's no logical reason for investment-phobia. But since it exists, it must be addressed, because confrontation is the best way to deal with any human fear, whether it's fear of flying, fear of crowds, or fear of finance.

First, the fear has to be recognized for what it is. There's nothing intrinsically scary about finance. For the most part, what we're really talking about is fear of the unknown, because, for many women, finance and investing signify the unknown.

Most people are afraid when they try something new. Opening the door to a dark room is scary—you don't know what's inside. Kids have been afraid of the dark ever since there have been kids and darkness. Taking your first airplane trip, starting a new job, being alone after years of depending on someone else—all of these can be scary, too.

It's not that men don't fear the unknown. They do. This kind of fear is universal. But for men, finance isn't the unknown. Finance has been their playing field for years. They wrote the script, they invented the lingo, they created the rules.

For most women, however, it's virgin territory, and so they often resist. They don't want to know, they want someone else to take care of it, they back away.

But finance isn't difficult. Back in the land of Oz, the Wizard ruled all-powerful until, thanks to Dorothy, his curtain fell, leaving only a little man in the corner manipulating those big levers. Finance is no more frightening than that small man. Like Dorothy, when you look beyond the curtain, you won't see a thing you can't handle.

Since the best way to overcome a fear is to deal with it head on, one of my goals is to help women face this issue so that they'll become realistic about investing. By doing so, they can grow less frightened about the investment world, and about their money in general. The fact that I knew absolutely nothing about money at the age of 40 and now, at 57, I run my own investment company should give you some encouragement. It can be done.

And the best way to begin is to start this minute. You don't have to be an expert to invest, but if you know some of the fundamentals, you can ask the experts the right questions.

Liz

At 53, Liz is happily married, with three grown children living in other states. She and her husband Tom both hold full-time jobs—Tom is a travel agent, and Liz, a social worker. Together they pull in $55–$65,000 a year, although this figure fluctuates due to the uncertainties of Tom's business.

Liz and Tom share their finances, and together have saved $200,000. Both sets of parents have passed away—it was an inheritance that gave them half of their savings. The couple also have IRAs and 401(k)s totaling $50,000 between them, and no other prospect for retirement money, except Social Security. Now that the kids are off on their own, Liz, who's bored with her work, wants to learn about finance, and hopes to be as involved as possible in her investment.

The first thing I told Liz was that she shouldn't quit her job to manage her money: There wasn't enough there to justify the loss of her salary, and it wouldn't require that kind of time anyway. Her evenings and weekends were perfectly suited to learning more about investments, if that's what she wished to do.

We then analyzed her finances in more detail. It turned out that she and Tom owned their house outright; they bought it thirty years ago for $39,000; today it's worth $150,000.

"Is the two hundred thousand dollars money you need to tap into?" I asked.

"No," Liz said. The couple live out in the farther suburbs, where the cost of living is lower than in the city.

Tom also has $50,000 worth of life insurance through his work, but since their total estate was too small to be taxed, I didn't recommend that they buy any more—the kids will inherit the money tax-free as it is. "Why not use that money now?" I asked. "Make it grow for you."

I did recommend they take $20,000 out of their savings and put it into something liquid for an emergency fund, leaving $180,000. At the moment Liz had it all in a balanced growth-and-income mutual fund, which had been earning her an average of about 10 percent a year.

Liz then mentioned something that was bothering her—several friends claimed that they were making much more on their investments than Liz; moreover, she had read a magazine article about a group of investors making 30–35 percent returns.

I cautioned her. "You don't want to get too aggressive," I said. "Your net worth isn't large enough to afford that luxury."

"But other people are making so much more money," she said.

"Yes," I said, "but those people making that kind of money can afford more risk than you can. Don't listen to those stories. You've been smart so far. You're making between nine and thirteen percent a year and that's very good."

Liz simply isn't in the category of those who belong in aggressive alternative investments, because she doesn't have enough capital to risk and she's too old to recover from a significant market loss. Liz needs steady growth. Her fund has done well for her each year, and if she wants to add something new, we could diversify her money a little more.

"Be disciplined instead," I said. "Why risk your future?"

Liz understood the point—the last thing she wanted to do was lose her savings. But she still wanted a little more risk. So we decided to take 25 percent out of her mutual fund and place it in three different, more aggressive funds.

Still, the bulk of Liz's money belongs in a diversified bond and equity portfolio. The fact is, I told her, there aren't that many things she can do with this kind of money. If Liz and Tom were to end their working days with $400,000, that would provide them with around $32,000 a year (plus Social Security) before any taxes.

Unnecessary risk is never a good idea, and while there are many women whom I urge to take more risk than they do, I would never dream of jeopardizing anyone's security. *The first rules of investing are protect principal and cover your down side.*

Liz is looking for nice, steady growth for the next dozen years. At some point, if she and Tom sell their house, they'll have that much more money to live on, too—assuming that housing values continue to hold, although it means living in a rental rather than in their own house.

"Isn't your goal to be secure later?" I asked Liz. "Then you better not throw the dice now."

Because Liz was still genuinely interested in learning more about investing, I recommended that, once she had exposed herself to financial markets and got some experience, she could manage some of her own money with the help of a good broker, but until then she should leave it to professional fund managers.

◆ ◆ ◆

A good investment strategy depends on a wide range of factors, including your age, your income level, and the amount of money you have to invest. Maybe you've just received a huge raise, or inherited a lump sum, or perhaps a divorce settlement arrived. Or maybe you just started working last year and you've already saved $2,500.

But no matter how young you are, and no matter where your money comes from, you should start saving and investing as soon as possible. The earlier you begin, the greater your success will be at the end.

The amount of money you start with isn't important. As you'll see in the section on retirement (see page 161), time is one of the most important factors in accumulating wealth, because time allows your money to compound.

This is a lesson you're almost never too young to learn. I began teaching my granddaughter Jessica about money when she was five years old, and she's learned enough to save her tooth money regularly. A few days ago she counted it up and told me that she was "loaded." But even if you're 55, it's not too late to start.

So let's say that, as of today, you have enough to begin investing.

Up until now you've probably been keeping your money in a money market account, or a bank. It's time for something different.

Not that each woman will or should take the same course. While I do recommend that you learn to be responsible for your money, not everyone needs to devote the same amount of attention and time to it. Some women are well suited for an in-depth investment education, and they'll want to take part in every decision. Others may want only to understand the fundamentals well enough to select an appropriate investment adviser. Either way, you'll need some knowledge of how to handle your assets.

First, what *are* assets?

There are four principal types of assets: **stocks, bonds, cash** (or cash equivalents), and **real estate.** (There are also assets which tend to be more speculative, such as commodity-type investments, including oil or gas; or nonfinancial investments, including precious and nonprecious metals; or fine art, coins, and other collectibles. This isn't the time to introduce speculative investments into a portfolio. These are for an expert's hand.)

Real estate is not always the best investment for a beginner because it's an **illiquid** asset. (**Liquidity** means that you can get your money quickly. For example, if your money is in a checking account, you can just write a check to withdraw it. That's liquid. If your money is illiquid, you can't get cash for it without some effort.)

The most obvious way to invest in real estate is to buy a home so you can live in it. That way, you can take advantage of the terrific tax deductions of a mortgage, and you get to have a home, too. With any luck, your home will increase in value. Time is on your side if you live in your home, because the odds are good that you'll stay there for years—which gives the house more time to appreciate in value. This approach is much less risky than buying a house just so you can turn around and sell it. That's called **speculation,** and to me speculating in real estate is like playing with an elephant—it's just too damn big to move quickly if the market turns the wrong way.

The problem is that you can lose your entire investment when the real estate market drops, because of what I call the **80/20 leverage**

factor. In other words, let's say that you've bought a $100,000 house; to do it, you had to make a down payment of $20,000. You owe the bank $80,000. Now, if, for some reason, you have to sell your house, and at the same time real-estate values have dropped, you can lose your $20,000, because the house may now only be worth $80,000, which is what you owe. Presto! Your money's gone.

Don't misunderstand me. Real estate has a place in your general portfolio, but until you have lots of liquid assets, even a home may not be your best first investment.

After real estate, we're left with stocks, bonds, and cash.

Basically, **stocks** are necessary for **growth, bonds** are necessary for **income,** and **cash** is necessary for **liquidity.**

Cash and cash equivalents are liquid, low in risk, and low in return. They include checking accounts, certificates of deposit (CDs), and money market accounts.

It's always good to have three to six months' worth of living expenses liquid. But there's no firm and fast rule that applies to everyone. Sure, having that kind of money around is helpful, but one medical bill, one dog with a broken leg, or one new car can eat up much of that money in a gulp. Conventional wisdom also says that people without regular paychecks, especially writers, artists, and other creative types, should try to keep enough cash on hand to cover at least a full year of expenses.

But if you do have enough money put aside for emergencies, and then more to spare, you can now become an investor.

Bank CDs and checking accounts are insured by the Federal Deposit Insurance Corporation (FDIC) up to $100,000 per account. If your bank collapses, the FDIC will make sure you don't lose your money up to that limit.

That's safety. Now, let me explain what financial risk means.

There are several ways in which you're paid for taking risks, because it is precisely by being willing to take some risks through investments that you earn money.

For example, there is **time risk.**

Let's say that you're willing to lock your money into a bond and then leave it alone for thirty years. (This is, by the way, a type of investment I dislike, but I'll tolerate it here for the learning experience.) You don't have a clue what the market will be like in thirty years. And you don't know about inflation either: Your money could be worth more if you hadn't locked it into this three-decade-long investment. So the fact that you're willing to put your money away for such a long time ought to reward you with a higher return than if the investment had been for only a few months. And it generally does: For instance, a long-term bond pays a higher interest rate than a short-term bond.

Besides time, another kind of risk is **business risk.**

If you've put your money into an investment that's subject to the ebbs and flows of normal business activity, you ought to be rewarded for that, too. Therefore you can make much more from investing with a private company, for instance, than you can investing with the United States government.

A third type of risk is **market risk,** as represented by the stock market's frequent ups and downs. The day after you've invested in a stock or bond, the price will most likely change for the better or worse, even if it's just by a fraction. Except for cash equivalents, all investments share some degree of change, or **volatility.** If you're willing to tolerate this kind of roller coaster and still sleep at night, you should be rewarded here, too.

In July 1996, the market had a crazy week, declining 161 points in one day, and then dropping another 85 the next day before finally rising. Unlike business risk, where a stock falls because the business itself has done poorly, here stocks fell because the entire market was falling. Of all my clients, only one was so scared that she called to say, "Sell!" But I said, "Then get yourself another money manager, because I won't sell based on one bad moment in the market." (My client eventually did calm down, and her stocks rose to their previous level, along with her mood.) Likewise, in 1977, the market was down 247 points on Friday, August 15, and then up 109 points the following Monday, and up another 115 points on Tuesday.

There are other, more sophisticated risks, including **currency risk** (investing in another country's currencies), or **country risk** (investing in securities outside the United States). But these risks are for investors who, if they lose some of their investment, will still have plenty of money left.

All these risks are the source of making money.

Now let's discuss the two principal investments: bonds and stocks.

What is a **bond?**

A bond is basically a certificate that says you've lent somebody money. It's the formal equivalent of a handwritten IOU.

One good way to understand a bond is to compare it to a mortgage. If you own your own home, your debt is your mortgage. It's the equivalent to a bond that you issued. You borrowed a certain number of dollars from the bank, and in return you've promised to pay a certain percent in interest every month and to repay it in full in, let's say, fifteen or thirty years. If you don't follow through, the bank can take your house, and that's called **secured debt.** There are also secured bonds, secured by assets such as real estate.

Now, if you lend money, how much should you be paid? That depends on who you lend it to.

Let's say that you decide to lend a small amount of money to your neighbor. You've known her all your life, you understand why she's borrowing the cash, and you know she has a job and a cash flow. You also know this loan represents a temporary need, and you trust that your neighbor will not only pay you back, but will also make regular interest payments. In return, you'll probably charge her a small interest rate. This loan doesn't feel like a big risk.

If that neighbor were the U.S. Treasury, for instance, the risk that you won't get your money back, or your interest, is minimal. The United States is a good credit risk. It deserves your trust, and so you won't ask for much in return. Little risk brings little reward.

But let's say you don't know your neighbor well. Her work record is sketchy, she doesn't have a steady job, and you're not sure about her cash flow. Personally, I wouldn't lend her anything, but if you really wanted to, you'd charge her a much higher rate of interest, as well as ask for her emerald ring as collateral.

The same is true for companies. A small company that hasn't been in business a long time, that doesn't have a steady track record of earnings, and that has limited assets would have to pay you more interest to persuade you to lend them money.

The more risk you take, the more interest you deserve.

How do you know how much risk you're taking? The best way is to look at such well-regarded agencies as **Standard & Poor's,** or **Moody's,** which rate bond-issuing companies. Standard & Poor's top rating is AAA, then AA and A, going down to D. Moody's ratings start at Aaa, then Aa and A, and go down to Ca. These ratings show you how safe your potential investment is.

Your creditors' creditworthiness determines how much you should get for lending them money.

Bonds are also called **fixed income** instruments, because they pay you a fixed amount of money on a regular basis, usually every six months, for the bond's life—unless the company goes out of business.

What would a bond look like? Think of a rectangle. A bond certificate is for a certain amount, such as $10,000. This is called the **face value,** and it's printed across the bond. The bond will also state the duration for which you're investing your money, which is called the **maturity date.** That's the specific day on which it is due. Maturity dates run from six months to a year all the way up to thirty years. The bond will also say that, until it matures, you will receive interest payments at the rate of, let's say, 7 percent per year, at an established frequency, such as annually, semiannually, or quarterly, unless the company undergoes a bankruptcy or a major restructuring.

(This interest rate is sometimes referred to as a **coupon,** because years ago coupons were attached to the bond certificates and people would bring these to the bank to cash them in. Today you don't receive any paper at all—everything is electronic.)

Remember, liquidity is basically the capacity to get immediate cash. A related term is **marketability,** which means that you can resell your investment *for* cash.

Most bonds are marketable. In other words, even if you've bought a ten-year bond, you don't have to hold on to it for the entire ten years. Very few people's lives are so stable that they'll want to hold on to a bond for such a long time. Things change. You suddenly find yourself with a new set of twins, or you've lost your job, or a relative needs a loan.

So you might think about selling your bond.

In order for bonds to change hands, they must have a price, just like anything else that you buy and sell. If that price is exactly the same as the face value—you buy a $10,000 bond for $10,000—that means you are buying it at what is called **par.** You're paying no more and no less than what you will get at its maturity. But let's continue with other options for this particular $10,000 bond with its 7 percent interest rate, which matures in ten years.

Whenever you listen to the news, it always seems someone's talking about the impact of interest rates on the economy, and especially on the price of bonds. What this means is: If one year after you bought your bond, bonds maturing at the same time as yours now pay 6 percent—and yours is paying 1 percent more—you can sell it for more than you paid for it.

If the price of your bond will be more than 100 percent of its face value, you're selling it at a **premium.**

So here is a second source of making money with your bond. The first is the interest you make from it. The second is selling the bond for what's known as a **capital gain.**

However, the reverse can also happen. Take the same scenario, except that this time the other bonds maturing when yours does are paying 8 percent. So, if you have to sell your 7 percent bond, people will give you less than $10,000 for it. The other person is buying your bond at what is known as a **discount.**

Let's talk about something else you've also heard countless times: interest rates are going up, or interest rates are going down, and as a result, the Fed is tightening; or, the Fed is loosening.

The Federal Reserve Board (or, as most people call it, the Fed) is an independent agency created in 1913 to monitor, influence, and manage the availability of money in the economy.

Simply put, when the Fed lowers interest rates, it becomes cheaper to borrow. Then, as people consume more, and companies increase their prices because there is demand, the economy expands, or heats up. Things cost more.

This is called **inflation.**

When inflation occurs, the Fed intervenes by raising short-term interest rates in order to slow down inflation.

By doing this, the Fed has basically made the price of borrowing money higher: It has become more expensive to borrow.

Like everything else, money has a price. Let's say that, as a company, you pay a 7 percent interest rate to your bondholders. This is more expensive for you than if you could pay them 6 percent. The interest rate on your bond is the cost of money to the company issuing the bond.

So if the Fed raises the price of money, people borrow less, because it's more expensive to borrow. Therefore they consume less too, and do less business. And therefore, it's slowed down inflation.

As an investor, you need to be aware of this movement, although you may not need to be aware of all the details. (Plus, you can talk about all this at a cocktail party and sound smart.)

So even if you don't remember why it's true, keep in mind that when interest rates fall, the value of your bond holdings rises. When interest rates rise, the value of your bond holdings falls.

When interest rates are rising, you want to be careful of long-term bonds. But normally I recommend you invest serially anyway, i.e., in staggered maturities of varying years. That way you'll be getting back money every year, and you can reinvest that money at different rates, allowing you to average your rate over time, and that helps defeat the chance for a loss.

What I don't recommend is to hold on to your money while you sit still praying for interest rates to go up so that you'll invest at a good rate. That way you may never get around to buying anything.

Bonds can be issued by anyone who is deemed creditworthy—the government and its agencies, states, municipalities, foreign countries, and companies all over the world. Most of this universe is rated by those agencies already mentioned.

There's a line in the bond ratings that separates what's considered higher-quality investments from lower-quality investments. That line is called a Triple B by Standard & Poor's, or BBB. Above that line bonds are considered **investment grade.** Below that line they are called **high-yield bonds.** The difference is that an investment-grade bond is of better quality, but pays less interest than the lower grade.

In other words, if GM issues bonds—or debt—this year, it may pay an 8 percent rate. But if the WXY Widget Company issues bonds, and it's a new company with a short track record of earnings, they might have to pay an interest rate of 10 percent. If you're not a sophisticated investor, and you want to buy these higher-risk, lower-rated bonds for their higher yields, please use a professional or a mutual fund to do so. This is one arena where it's easy to get burned. You really need good research.

◆ ◆ ◆

The other common asset class is **stocks.**

The relationship between you, the stockholder, and the company that issued the stock is profoundly different from the relationship you had with your bond issuer. When you bought a bond, someone owed you money. This isn't true with stocks. Generally speaking, when you buy a stock, you aren't guaranteed any income at all. You're not even guaranteed that you'll get your money back.

A stock is the certificate of your ownership of a certain proportion of the company. This is also called **equity.**

Stocks are sold via a stock market. The market always reminds me of an electrocardiogram. It's like your own ticker. You watch it go up and down, and up and down. As long as it goes up more than down, you're okay. The difference is that a flat line on an EKG means you're dead; with a stock, it just means that your money isn't going anywhere, which, if everyone else's is going up, is pretty bad, too.

If you were to graph the market's history, you'd find that people often buy stocks when the market goes up, and they sell when it goes down. This is such a powerful intuitive temptation that nearly everyone falls into this trap. It's the herd mentality at work.

But is this your image of yourself? Do you want to think of yourself as mutton? A few year ago, going across town in a New York City taxicab, the driver turned around and told me to sell a certain stock, because he'd heard it was going down. Well, I say, it's time to *buy* when cabbies are telling you to sell. (I also told him to watch the road rather than me.) The market was gloomy at that time, but sure enough, it eventually rebounded, and people who bought at that time did very well for themselves, while people who sold, lost. That cabby is probably still driving a cab, if he's lucky.

Instead of behaving like a sheep, stick to a good balanced basic investment plan, and leave it alone. Few people can pull off what's known as **market timing**—buying or selling a stock based on the belief that the stock market is about to go up or down. Investing is a little like baking. Of course, I've never been able to make a soufflé in my life, but I've been told that if you keep opening the oven door to check it, it will fall. In other words, don't keep changing your original plan.

When you buy a stock, you invest in the fate of the company (business risk). You're also investing in the market, since the market alone can take a stock up or down (market risk). It has its own momentum. The market can even be considered emotional. It rises and falls on events. Has war been declared? Has the president been shot? The market will drop. Your company can be doing well, and even so, in a crash like 1987's, everything goes down: the good, the bad, and the excellent, too.

You must live through these events. They won't hurt you for long.

Also, when you're ready to buy stock, you'll see that people classify them in different ways, including **large capitalization, small capitalization, growth companies,** and **blue-chip companies.** Some of these classifications are made by the value of a corporation, determined by multiplying the number of outstanding shares by the current market price of a share. **Large-capitalization (large-cap) stocks** are those calculated at over three billion dollars of outstanding market value, while **small-capitalization (small-cap) stocks** come in at under $250 million. (Mid-cap companies are those that fall between large and small.) **Growth companies** are those that have exhibited faster-than-average gains in earnings over the last few years, and are expected to continue to show high levels of profit growth. These stocks are usually riskier investments than average stocks, however, and therefore offer less assurance of long-term return. **Blue-chip stocks** are those of nationally known companies with long records of profit growth and dividend payment, as well as a reputation for quality management, products, and services. These stocks tend to be higher priced, and generally tend to be large-cap.

In order to attract capital, some companies pay **dividends** to their stockholders, which means that they share a portion of their profits with you as they grow. A dividend is like an interest payment that the company pays you out of its earnings. The amount and frequency of the dividends paid are at the discretion of the company, however, and you're not guaranteed any money in any way. In fact, you often don't even know if the company will pay you any dividends at all.

Another kind of stock is called **preferred stock,** which is something of a mix between stocks and bonds. These pay dividends, so they create income like bonds, but they also have the capacity to appreciate, more like a stock. On the down side, the dividend isn't increased if the company makes profits, and the price of preferred stock moves more slowly than that of common stock.

Once you buy stock, you become a shareholder, and a part-owner of the company. Since I bought my granddaughter Jessica some Toys 'Я' Us stock, she likes to tell people that the store belongs to her. It took me some time to explain that she didn't own the whole store, but a very small part. Still, she walks through its corridors like a proud proprietor. Maybe she's looking for the part she owns.

Unlike a bond, a stock's key feature is its price. You need to know the number of shares that you've bought and the price at which you bought them.

Also unlike a bond, with a stock you aren't guaranteed anything. If business is bad, the company can stop paying a dividend, and a bond can default. If it's good, they can increase it.

Now that you've bought your stock, the next step is to allow the market to evaluate it. Most stocks are readily marketable, that is, they can be sold easily. But since stocks go up and down, the stock's resale depends on its price the moment you wish to sell it. If this happens to be on a day when the market is booming, there's a good chance you'll sell it for a good price. If it's a depressed day, you'll probably see less for it.

Even though your stock may go up in price, you don't realize your gains—or your losses—until you actually sell.

You could buy a stock for $1,000, for instance, and watch it drop in value to $500, then see it rise again to $2,000. But since you haven't done anything with the stock during this time, this is called a **paper loss,** or a **paper gain,** and it's something that you don't need to follow closely. Traders monitor these movements, looking for as little as one-sixteenth of a point—but we're not traders. We're looking to build our net worth over time and grow our capital by having a prudent, smart investment plan with long-term goals and a view to the future.

That's why a philosophical view of stocks is important: Invest in the right companies, then sit back and allow them to evolve. Let the market do its thing.

◆ ◆ ◆

To summarize, your possible investments include stocks and bonds, cash equivalents, and your home, if you can afford one. Avoid investing every nickel you own, however, because you don't want to be forced to sell your long-term investments in an emergency. There you are, doing well enough, when, all of a sudden, the stock market dips down just when you need a new car and college tuition. You must keep enough cash around so that you don't need to sell your stocks when prices are down.

The very least you want to do with your money is keep up with inflation. Historically women have tended to believe that inflation is some abstract notion that doesn't really affect anyone; just one of those mathematical terms floating around in the air. So some inflation index went up 4 percent. Big deal.

But the truth is, if you keep adding that 4 percent up over the years, you can see that this isn't a joke. In just five years of 4 percent inflation, $100 sinks to being worth less than $83. Another way to understand inflation is to think of a glass of water sitting on a table. If you don't touch the glass over time, the water will slowly evaporate, and you'll have less and less, even if you've never taken a single sip.

The same is true of your money. You'll have less and less purchasing power.

What you earn on your money after inflation is what's known as your **real return.** So even if your money market account is paying you 3 percent, if inflation is also 3 percent, you haven't gained purchasing power. After you pay taxes on the 3 percent interest, you've actually lost money.

So you want to do more than keep all your money in a CD or a Treasury bill, because CDs and T-bills, over time, pay interest that equals only the rate of inflation.

Over the years longer-term, investment-grade bonds have beaten inflation by almost 2 percent. That's not a great deal, but these bonds pay you on a regular basis, so if you require income and are risk-averse, they may well be a prudent investment. But they're fairly low risk, so you won't make a lot of money—they'll pay you just a little more than a CD.

For real growth, your primary vehicles are stocks. And this is as it should be: You're not just lending to someone for a short time and then taking it back; as a stockholder, you're putting your money to work in the active economy, and the active economy appreciates that. The real return on Standard & Poor's 500 largest-company stocks over the long term has been 7 percent (10 percent minus 3 percent inflation).

Small-company stocks have returned an average of an extra couple of percentage points over the S&P 500 large stocks. But they're riskier, and so it's only fair that they should pay you even more than the large-company stocks over the long run.

◆ ◆ ◆

As I've mentioned, many women are afraid to go near the stock market. They agree with my father who, thinking that investing in stocks was a form of betting, bet on dice instead. But the difference between the two is that when you play craps, you're depending solely on luck. When you choose a stock, you rely on good research, sound knowledge, and proven strategies.

As far as I know, the best of the approaches for making money consistently is called **diversification.** This is a concept we've been hearing all our lives in different words, addressing many different subjects, and those words are: Don't put all your eggs in one basket.

You reach diversification in investing through careful **asset allocation,** which means distributing your investment dollar among different investment (asset) classes.

The principal asset classes discussed can be broken down into more specific classes, such as by economic sector, by region, by quality, and so on.

To make sure that you aren't tied to one particular area, you want to spread your investments around. You want to buy some conservative securities and you want others that give you growth. You may want some investments in one part of the world, and some in another. You should have stocks in different industries, too, even though they may appear to have more risk attached. Just by making sure that your investments are spread over a range of options, you're taking an enormously important step toward guaranteeing your success.

A simple way to start asset allocation is through what I call the **institutional asset allocation,** a formula used by most pension funds and balanced mutual funds. This consists of a portfolio composed of 60 percent stocks and 40 percent bonds, in addition to whatever cash you have. It's a simple and rational method that gives you some income, through the bonds, and some growth, through the stocks.

It's a constant tradeoff, growth and income, income and growth. When you want income, you often give up growth. When you want growth, you don't get as much income.

Not that this formula always works for everyone. Sometimes we run into women who truly need income, but if they don't grow their money, they won't be able to take care of themselves in their accustomed style. So we have to put more of their portfolio into stocks than is really comfortable. It's important to be realistic. Your portfolio can't always be the theoretical ideal, because it has to suit your individual purposes.

◆ ◆ ◆

Knowing now that you have to think about diversifying, your next step is to consider actually buying something.

The three fundamental alternatives are: individual bonds and individual stocks, both of which we've discussed, and **mutual funds.** Or, if you have $200,000 or more, it might be worthwhile hiring an **asset manager** (which we'll talk about shortly).

There are more than 7,000 mutual funds as of this moment, and by the time you read this, there may be a few hundred more, while some of the existing ones will have closed. Basically, these mutual funds are pools of assets, or investors' money, managed by a particular manager or team that uses a clearly defined and publicly disclosed investment policy, and is registered through the Securities and Exchange Commission.

The vehicle through which the fund manager discloses her plans to the public is called a **prospectus.**

Don't buy a fund without reading this prospectus—or at least, without having your adviser look at it with you. I often hear women say, "I didn't know the fund cost an extra two percent a year," or, "I didn't know the manager could buy speculative investments." But everything the fund managers are permitted to do is in the prospectus. It may be in teeny-weeny print, so don't just read the bold letters—that's the come-on stuff. Ignore the pretty pictures of the Statue of Liberty or Mount Rushmore and read the fine print. Some funds automatically reinvest your dividends, and maybe you'd prefer to have the cash. Other funds may charge you money to reinvest those dividends, and you don't want that either. Read everything beforehand, or don't complain later.

As an investor, when you buy a mutual fund, you're buying units, or shares, of this particular pool; you're now a holder of a certain proportion of the investments of this pool.

Every day the fund manager has to mark her portfolio to market, which means that she prices the shares to whatever they're worth that day, divides that price by the number of units sold to the public, and publishes how much each unit is worth. This is called the **net asset value** of a fund. You can look it up in the paper and check the value of your mutual-fund unit. Or your broker can tell you. You'll be sent a regular statement, too.

There are different ways to buy funds. Some are called **open-end** funds, and some are **closed-end.** Open-end funds take money every day. You can buy into the fund, or liquidate your units daily, at the net asset value. Closed-end funds have a fixed number of shares which are usually listed on a major stock exchange and cannot be liquidated as easily.

One of a mutual fund's greatest advantages is that you're relieved from making detailed investment decisions, leaving you only with the choice of which asset classes to put your money into, such as stocks, or bonds, or subclasses, or combinations of these.

You aren't involved in choosing the actual **security** (which means bonds or stocks). The fund manager does that for you, and since the pool holds a large amount of money, it can diversify more and protect you more than you could with your own $10,000. True, $10,000 worth of stocks and bonds buys you a few positions, but in a mutual fund it can give you many positions, because you own a small piece of a big pool of investments.

Another advantage of a fund is that you don't have to be a genius to prosper. Fund managers are professionals who spend all their time reading and analyzing the market so that you don't have to. If I have an elbow pain, I wouldn't buy a book to figure out how to make it feel better. I'd go to a doctor who understands joints. Even if you can't afford to learn finance yourself, or hire an adviser, you can afford a mutual fund, which gives you that kind of assistance.

The range of mutual funds is extensive. Most funds stick to a certain specialty, such as large cap stocks, growth stocks, municipal bonds, high-yield junk bonds, foreign stocks, or even gold and silver. Others create balanced mixes. Some sell directly to the consumer, some charge sales fees and sell through brokers or other agents.

Thus you can pick a fund in any of the asset classes in which you've decided to invest. Or better yet, pick a few, and diversify yourself right from the start. In other words, allocate your money yourself, putting perhaps 45 percent into a bond fund, 20 percent into a large-capitalization stock fund, 15 percent into a small-cap stock fund, 10 percent into a foreign stock fund, and the remaining 10 into two others that you've heard about and like.

Many mutual-fund companies sell their units directly to consumers without using intermediaries and without charging fees. There are always management expenses, however, and these are disclosed in the fund's annual report. The price of the unit, the net asset value, is published every day and calculated after taking into account these management fees and expenses.

When you buy directly from the fund, you are generally purchasing what is called a **no-load** fund. This means there are no major fees other than the fund's management costs, which are reflected in the net asset value.

As mentioned, many fund companies employ intermediaries. These intermediaries have to make money also, so you incur additional expenses by using them.

These intermediaries once were solely brokerages, but now they also include banks, investment advisers, insurance companies, etc. In return for a fee or commission they offer you recommendations on which funds to buy and sell, as well as managing the process for you. **Loads,** or fees, can range from $^3/_4$ of a percent to 8 percent, and by law they must be disclosed to you.

These fees can be **front load,** indicating that you pay right away; or **back end,** meaning that you pay when you sell the fund units; or **level load,** which means that the fee is deducted regularly from the value of your shares. Some funds use a combination of all three, so watch out.

For the most part, the no-load fund companies offer you no advice, although this custom is changing. But generally, no-load means no advice and no fee, and load means advice with a fee.

Now consider this: If you invest $100 in a 5 percent front-load fund, out of $100 you're actually investing only about $95. So, after a nice yearly return of 10 percent, instead of making $10, you've made 10 percent of $95, or $9.50. Thus you may feel obliged to stay in this investment for several years in order to amortize your load—in other words, to spread the cost of the 5 percent sales charge over time, to make up for the money you spent in year one.

Similarly, you may not want to sell a back-end fund for a long time, because you don't want to pay the fee. And this may color the way you handle your investments, and it certainly can affect your return.

So the load can influence your money-making capability, as well as your psychology.

Beyond that, here's something else to remember: We're all human beings. That same intermediary who last year sold you a fund with a 5 percent front load may tell you this year to buy a different one. It's not his money, after all, and he gets a new commission. You must be alert when you're operating in the load arena. Otherwise, you may find yourself paying out more in fees than is worthwhile.

◆ ◆ ◆

Let's talk more about the concept of letting other people handle your money.

For many of you, paying full attention to your investments is out of the question. You're too busy. There's nothing wrong with asking a broker to carry out your transactions for you: It's no different than having any other professional in your life.

There are a few factors to consider, however.

First, let's look at the concept of **discretion.** When you give a stockbroker discretion, you're letting her buy or sell a stock without having to tell you about each transaction when she makes it (she will always send you a confirmation at a later date). This doesn't mean that she can take money out of your account. It means that she can buy and sell in your account. She is now your portfolio manager.

You must investigate this person's reputation and her track record before handing over your discretion. Get to know her. Ask questions. Watch how she eats. Seriously. Henry Ford once said that he'd never hire anyone until they had a meal together, where he'd watch to see if his prospective employee salted his food before he tasted it. If he did, no job.

Disreputable people populate every industry, and this one is no exception, but if you do your homework and are at a good firm with a good reputation, the odds are in your favor.

If you feel your broker isn't serving you well, you can always talk to her office manager, as well as the company's compliance officer, who ensures that the firm obeys the rules set by the Securities and Exchange Commission (SEC) and the National Association of Securities Dealers (NASD). You can also call the NASD hot line at (800) 289-9999.

Equally important, you must be honest with yourself. If you're planning on devoting time to your investments, then enjoy it. But if you're kidding yourself, you'll run into trouble. The other day I was talking to a woman who was complaining bitterly that her broker had sold a friend's stock in a certain company, but not hers. But then she admitted that she hadn't given the man discretion, so when he hadn't been able to reach her after many calls, he wasn't legally allowed to sell it. "Too bad," I said. The woman had lost $10,000, and she had no one to blame but herself. She should have returned her broker's call, or hired someone she trusted and given him discretion.

Don't give your broker discretion if you don't mean it. If every trade she makes upsets you and you tell her, "I didn't really want you to buy that," or "I didn't really want you to sell that," you're doing no one a service. If you keep it up, your broker may end up firing you.

Even if you do give your broker full discretion, you must check in with her every three to six months. And read your statements carefully. So many women say, "Don't make me read that piece of paper with all the numbers on it." If you feel you won't understand, then have your broker help you with it. It's not that complicated. And it is your money.

Read your **stock-trade confirmations,** too. Don't tell me you didn't know your broker bought you such-and-such a stock and that you hate that kind of stock and wish she hadn't done it. The only reason you didn't know was that you didn't bother to open your mail and read the confirmation.

If you see something peculiar on the statement, ask. You get a physical every year, and if something odd turns up, you ask. If something odd happens to your money, ask. You can address a problem right away, if you're paying attention. Otherwise, the problem may grow.

Another factor to consider in selecting the right broker is objectivity: You want someone to choose investments impartially. Make sure that she isn't just selling you her own firm's products, nor should she be bound by a limited array of options within her own firm.

And keep in mind the structure of her compensation. If she's earning commissions from your investments, that may color her advice. Also, she'll be receiving no commissions when she's doing nothing— i.e., neither buying nor selling anything for you. Yet there are many times when doing nothing is exactly the right course of action, sometimes for very long periods of time.

When I entered the business as a stockbroker, I was trained to sell, not to invest. Brokers are essentially salespeople. So ask yourself some questions when you meet. Is this someone who listens to your questions well enough to make you feel understood? Is she guiding you in your decisions, or just selling you products you don't really understand? What about the corporate culture of her company—does it have a sales culture, or is it research driven? You want the latter. How do you find out? Always the same answer: Ask. Ask other people who work with the company, ask your broker herself. And remember, check references, check security regulators—even the Internet has a site for investigating brokers.

◆ ◆ ◆

Let's say that you decide you need more than a stockbroker. Perhaps you would prefer to hire someone to manage your entire investment portfolio.

The major difference between a brokerage account and a money management account is that whenever your broker performs a transaction, you pay a commission. An asset manager, however, charges you a fee based on a percentage of the money under her management. She makes her money by performing well for you: The more money you make, the more she makes. The benefit here is that you always know your costs, because the fee is a constant percentage; it can range from $3/4$ of 1 percent to 3 percent, depending on the size of your account (the larger the account, the smaller the percentage fee).

You generally need $200,000 or more to hire an asset manager, although there are always exceptions.

When you first meet a manager—interview several to find one you like—try to understand her approach, her policy, her philosophy, her track record over the years. Make sure that she understands your objectives, time horizon, and expectations. In other words, is she listening to you or just trying to sell you?

Once you've made a selection, let her do her thing. You must maintain good communication, but you don't have to talk every day. Once every few months may be enough.

Another benefit of asset management is that you've reduced the broker's possible conflict of interest, because there are no transaction charges. That means she doesn't make money every time you buy or sell. Her incentive to do well derives from the percentage of your money that she receives as her fee. Your success is her success.

An asset manager is not necessarily preferable to a stockbroker. Hiring one is simply another way to take care of your money.

Altogether, you can find many outlets to manage your money with input from advisers, in different combinations, and under a variety of pricing arrangements. There are, for example, investment advisers who design and supervise a portfolio of investments, charging a percentage of assets as an annual fee. They may choose other money managers or brokers to work with, or they may manage the funds themselves. Some investment advisers, usually consultants, may charge an hourly fee; use them as you need them.

No arrangement relieves you of responsibility regarding your portfolio. You still need to study your quarterly statements. Try to become familiar with indexes (such as Standard and Poor's 500) that reflect average market movement. Few people make money when everyone else is losing money, but you don't want to lose money when everyone else is making it.

◆ ◆ ◆

Now that you've invested your money, how do you measure the performance of your investment? Through **benchmarks** and **standards of performance**.

There are now over a hundred years' worth of statistics on the

United States stock and bond markets. These numbers give investors a sense of history, allowing them to sense what the future may bring, and giving them something against which to measure their current performance.

For years I used to wonder, who is this Dow Jones guy? (After all, my brother once had a friend named Jim Beam.) All day on the radio I would hear Dow Jones this, Dow Jones that. I thought he was the busiest man in America. Finally I learned that Dow Jones is an index representing the composite average of thirty of the most influential large stocks on the New York Stock Exchange. When people speak about how the market's doing, they usually mean the daily Dow Jones Industrial Average.

There are plenty of other indexes too: There's one for the entire New York Stock Exchange; there's one for every sector, such as industrial stocks; there's one for every other market, such as the American Stock Exchange; as well as for European or Asian markets, bonds, over-the-counter stocks, and many more.

It's the claim of the advisory industry (those people who say they can best tell you how to invest, and what to invest in) that they can beat these averages. But the truth is that few people beat the markets on a consistent basis. Think about it: Zillions of investors all are trying to do the same thing, and there simply aren't that many bargains.

This doesn't mean you can't make money. It just means you can't expect to make unrealistic amounts of money.

Be wary of advisers who promise you numbers way out of historic ranges. A good adviser manages your expectations as well as she manages your money. This is an important factor to consider when making a choice. If your adviser focuses on the behavior of markets, and educates you on historical performance, and warns you that amazing returns can be had only with undue risk, then you've found a balanced person. If she guarantees you that she'll double your money in two years, tell her she's a genius, then run for the hills.

There's nothing intrinsically wrong with alternative investments, but because they involve much higher risk and offer much greater rewards, they're for people of some wealth. Most of you don't have to read this paragraph, but if you do have a great deal of money handy, then by all means you're in a position to put a percentage of your money into such investments as leveraged buyouts, private equity funds, hedge funds, distressed debt, and fallen angels. These have a high risk and a high reward. But I repeat, they're only for people of wealth. If you have $100,000 liquid net worth, and your broker tries to convince you to risk it on something that promises extraordinary returns, watch out! Don't buy into pie in the sky.

◆ ◆ ◆

If your adviser is wise, she will eventually know you well enough to assess your risk tolerance.

Your adviser must tell you what to expect, and what not to expect, in reaching your goals. And she's going to have to assess how you react to risk.

When you first start investing, you don't know how much risk you can take on and still sleep well at night. Perhaps you'll discover that you can't tolerate the risk necessary for your goals, and if so, your adviser is going to have to deal with that. Or she may tell you that you already have enough money, so that great risks aren't necessary, because your primary need is to preserve your capital rather than increase it. You and your adviser will eventually figure out how much risk you need to take, and how much you can stand.

Risk is a little like traveling. Some people like to walk, because they're afraid of driving. This is the equivalent of having a CD in the bank. Some people take more of a chance and drive on the highway, to get farther faster. This is like buying bonds. And some people take a plane. It can take you everywhere—and this is like having stocks. All investments vehicles are useful, but remember that some get you where you want to go a lot more quickly. And they do involve more risk.

Some women may read this and say, Do I really need to take risks? The answer is no—if, and only if, you have substantial wealth. I once talked to a woman with a net worth of more than $25 million. Her investment strategy is to buy only nice, safe Treasury bonds at a low interest rate. I don't agree with this decision, but this woman isn't going to starve.

You really won't know how you deal with risk until you take your first loss. One of my clients, five days after her first investment, said, "I'm up, I'm down, I can't stand it any longer. I have to get out of this." Five days, and she was ready to jump ship. Luckily, by the time she got her first statement, she was up, and agreed to stay put.

Forget the movement. You have to look three to five years ahead. Fluctuation doesn't mean a loss, and it shouldn't scare you, but many women I work with do get scared. I tell them to talk to me. I try to help them get over the fear. You don't need to be scared, even if your account is down. Everyone has a down cycle. The more you understand, the less afraid you'll become.

This brings up the concept of **margin.** During the 1987 crash, some people had to sell their stocks because they had used margin; in other words, to buy a dollar's worth of stock, these people had borrowed 50 cents, which is sort of like the mortgage on your house, except here you can borrow up to 50 percent to make purchases. But when the market goes down enormously, you will be required to put up more money on what you owe, and if you can't, you have to sell stock. Being forced to sell when prices have tanked is bad, which is why I don't recommend margin to people unless they're extremely wealthy and have the cash available to put up if they need it. Margin is the same as borrowing, and it really increases your risk. My only customer to lose money in the 1987 crash had bought on margin (or, as they say, she was highly **leveraged**), and she had to sell all her holdings. So the moral is: If you spend what you don't have, you may run into trouble.

If your first investment goes sour, don't let that be the mouse that scared the elephant. Look at me. I lost everything that first time. It didn't feel good, but it intrigued me. I saw how I did it wrong, and felt I could do it right.

Put time and attention into your basic investment education. Then let the markets work for you, and monitor the progress. Now you can learn to understand the world and its economy through your own investments. You'll see which factors affect which events. Investing will bring the world closer to you.

Judy's Investing No-nos:

- Don't take unnecessary chances, particularly during the early stages of investment. When your capital base is low, a risky investment that loses money is a disaster—it's much worse than not making a top return. Think about it: If today you have $1,000 and you're earning 5 percent, at the end of the year you'll have $1,050. If, however, you lose 5 percent, you have $950 at the year's end. So next year you're not starting with $1,000, but $950. Now if you make 5 percent of $950, you're not even catching up to where you were before—you'll only have $997.50.

- Don't invest just because you've read about a hot tip. For the most part, if this tip was in a magazine, it was already known to others many weeks before it was published, and the information is already reflected in the price of the security.

- Don't play the telephone game. When your friend Marge calls to say that her brother told her about a big buyout of WXY Company which he heard from his best friend who's a clerk at the company who overheard it in the men's room from the company's president who was talking on his cell phone, don't buy it. These kinds of tips aren't the way to make money. Not that people don't do it. In fact, it's so prevalent I call it black-line fever, all that noise over the telephone about do this, buy that, so-and-so says such-and-such is going out of business. Too many brokers and investors are gripped by this fever, lowering their voices and whispering confidentially into the telephone. It's always a great and wonderful secret, and one you can usually forget about.

- Don't try to time the market. Timing the market means that you're waiting for the Dow Jones to drop 140 points because you know it's too high, and because you're convinced it's going to fall—so why not just wait a few more months to invest your money? People who waited like that in the early 1990s are still waiting, while everyone else has made a bundle on their investments, because the stock market did extremely well during that period. Yes, the market will go down sometimes. Maybe it will go way down. But you don't know when, so don't pretend you do. Don't manipulate your investments with frequency. Don't react to news by jerking your portfolio around. Learn to make good, informed decisions. Stay put.

- Don't worry about what happens the first week you invest, and above all, don't react. You could buy and your stock might go up ten points soon, and that doesn't mean you're a genius. Nor does it mean you're a loser if it drops ten points. Just leave it. When you first made the decision to buy that stock, you must have had a good reason. Give it time.
- Don't get bamboozled by strangers on the phone. Someone who calls you out of the blue and says, "Have I got a deal for you," doesn't have a deal for you. He doesn't know you, he doesn't want to help you, and the best thing you can do is hang up.
- Don't lay all the responsibility for your money on your investment adviser. Watch your own account. Not for theft—in my experience that's a rarity. Watch it for performance, so that you know what's happening, in case you want to get out of this portfolio. You can't complain four years later with any justification if you weren't paying any attention today.
- Don't frown too much, or you'll get wrinkles.

Chapter 9

Working, and Planning What Happens After Work

You can be young without money, but you can't be old without it.
Tennessee Williams

*I*nterviewing for a job was excruciating.

First off, my entire wardrobe at the time consisted of shorts, T-shirts, and tennis outfits, so I went out and bought a white linen suit and white pumps. Then I cold-called people to set up a few meetings.

So different from life as I knew it, none of this seemed real. Me, calling people for a job? Couldn't be. This was some form of out-of-body experience, as though I were acting out a role in a 1980s version of Joan Crawford's *Mildred Pierce:* all dressed up in my good outfit, in the streets for the first time, telling my daughters hope lay beyond the horizon, looking for a job, feeling humiliated and silly, trying to hold back the tears and sound professional all at once.

The first men I met tried to take advantage of me. I told them why I wanted to become a broker, and they told me I didn't have enough experience. "But I've done so many other things," I said. They didn't hear that.

"Being a single mother is hard work," I tried. They didn't hear that, either.

I mentioned my friend's money. That they heard, and so they told me I could be a secretary, that they would manage my friend's money, and that they'd even allow me a tiny piece of the action. They smiled at one another as though they had the world's biggest hearts. I declined the offer.

Other companies wouldn't even let me show up for the interview. Some required a college degree to take their entry test. Some just weren't interested in anyone over 40, male or female, who had no college education or job experience.

At one firm I offered to work for free if they'd only train me. They declined.

Each night I'd come home, worn and worried, and try to convince myself that everything was just fine. After a bad night's sleep, I'd get up, put on that linen suit, and try again.

Finally I arranged a lunch with a successful female broker who was a friend of a friend. This was the closest I'd come to meeting a woman already doing what I hoped to do. My expectations never higher, I sat down and spilled out my guts to Jean, who was the consummate female professional, making me feel less than sure of myself in my make-believe working woman's outfit.

Through it all Jean listened attentively, but when I was done, she tried to change my mind. "This is a man's business," she said. "They're tough. They don't like women."

"I don't care," I said. Then she told me that my dress was too short. "Fine," I said. She continued with one comment after another, but I persisted until she rolled her eyes and offered me an interview at the company where she'd been working for many years. It wasn't one I had heard of: Drexel Burnham Lambert. Still, I was willing to go anywhere, meet with anyone, including Jean's assistant manager, Charlie.

This felt like my final chance. One slip and it was over. And from Jean's description, Charlie, an ex-Marine, sounded like an advertisement for raging testosterone. I went into the meeting determined to hold my own. How bad could one case of male hormone overload be?

Not bad at all, it turned out. For whatever reasons, Charlie turned out to be a decent man who took to me almost on sight. After a long conversation he started hinting he would help me get a job. "But you need a résumé," he said.

"What can I put in it?" I asked. "Twenty years' experience as a mom?"

He laughed, and introduced me to Brad, his manager, and following a quick and successful meeting, they decided to give me a shot in their sales training program starting in July 1982. After six months the program led to a test, and by passing the test, you joined the company. "I don't know why," Brad said, "but I want to give you a chance."

I almost cried. I had a career.

But the notion of a test terrified me. I'd never been a good student and, on top of that, a great deal of math was involved, and I didn't feel capable of memorizing all the formulas. I was also intimidated by the surroundings, with all these steely guys running around acting cocky and invulnerable.

But now I learned about the word *focus*. I knew this test was not a dress rehearsal, nor a movie. This was real life. I had decided that I couldn't fail, and I wasn't going to. I studied for that exam like there was no tomorrow—because if I didn't pass it, that's what I felt there would be.

Scared, I turned to a man for support. My relationship with the X-ray technician had ended, and now there was John, who'd entered my life after my operation when, because I couldn't drive, I had rented a limousine for Stacey's fourteenth birthday. When the car pulled up and the handsome owner-driver stepped out, Stacey yelled, "Mom, you've got to see this guy!" That was John.

We were only friends for many months, but once the X-ray technician was gone, John and I started dating. He'd cook, I'd study, and then we'd have fun.

At work I watched the markets, made a few trades, and my friend came through with his money. But I was also soliciting accounts, trying to bring in as much business as possible, although as a trainee I wasn't able to handle the accounts; Jean took care of the business for me.

In my third month Brad doubled my salary to $3,000 a month. To me, this was real money. Every time I got a paycheck I'd stare at it, looking at my name, the $3,000, and then my name again.

By the day of the test I was prepared but frightened. It was just as grueling as they had promised.

The results were due the Thursday following that Saturday, but I called in on Monday and refused to go to work. "No way," I told Brad. "I'm not coming in until the results come in."

I was too scared. My principal had dwindled to less than $50,000 and my horizon was empty. I began to envision the rest of my life standing behind a department-store perfume counter, spraying strangers for a living. "A little Chanteuse?" I would ask people. "You smell divine."

But I did pass the test—in fact, I received a ridiculously high score, due to my intense studying—and the world was spared the sight of me hawking fragrances.

Anna

Anna, at the age of 60, recently married for the third time. Including stocks, bonds, cash, and a fully owned $750,000 home, Anna is worth about $3 million, a small amount of this inherited from her recently deceased parents, and the bulk of it from her two divorces.

Anna's new husband was Scott, a handsome 45-year-old ex–tennis pro. His career netted him some money, but he went through it quickly and has little left. Still, Anna didn't ask for a prenuptial agreement. This startled me, but she claims that she simply hadn't thought about it, particularly since this was the first time she'd married someone who had less money than she did.

Anna's own money has been sitting with a broker with whom she's greatly dissatisfied: whenever they meet, the broker insists that Scott accompany her, whereupon he and the broker do most of the talking, causing Anna to feel left out, especially since they're talking about her money.

Anna's goal is to make sure that she doesn't have to work, and although she's willing to leave Scott some money, she wants her only child to inherit more.

I'm not a marriage counselor and I never give marital advice: My own experience hardly qualifies me. But I do know that even wonderful marriages can end, and money can create discord. So I told Anna to find a good lawyer and to look into setting up a living trust for herself, with all her assets to be held in that trust during her life.

"Aren't trusts for after you're dead?" Anna asked.

"No," I said. I told her she needed the trust to separate her assets from her husband's. Scott doesn't own anything that Anna held before their marriage, but if they were to commingle the money now, there's a possibility he might be able to claim it as his. This was the most important message for Anna: Don't commingle your funds, and establish a paper trail when and where your money was used.

"You've married three times," I said. "You may marry again. Do you want to give away half of your money in a divorce?"

What would happen if Scott married someone else after her? Would Anna want Scott's next wife to wear her jewelry, or buy a house from the money Scott received from Anna's estate? "Be a realist," I said. "That's your choice, to support him. But you must define what you think Scott needs, or what you feel good about giving him."

I also urged Anna to cover her assets with an umbrella insurance policy. It soon became obvious that Anna knew nothing about her insurance coverage, so I suggested she gather her papers and consult with an agent. And if the liability currently included in her home and auto insurance policies didn't add up to cover her $3 million, then the umbrella policy would carry the slack.

Once we resolved these issues, we then discussed investing Anna's money.

But first I wanted to know why her broker was talking to Scott rather than to her. For that Anna had no answer, except that the broker, who had worked with her last husband, never seemed to take her seriously. I told her that if her broker refused to be communicative, it was time for her to find someone else. Stockbrokers are in a service business, and it's their job to make you feel comfortable, not only with their performance, but with their relationship with you.

Anna's portfolio startled me. Her broker had invested Anna heavily in aggressive-growth stocks, which was all wrong. It represented one basic type of stock, meaning that Anna had no diversification, and it also stood for an aggressive approach that made no sense at all for Anna's life-style or future needs.

Anna lives on $100,000 a year, so she doesn't need to make more money. Her goal is to keep her principal intact and earn a decent return without taking much risk. Anna doesn't spend all of what she makes, so there's no real incentive for her to shoot for the moon with all growth stocks. I recommended instead that she consider a diversified portfolio allocated all over the board, but the basic breakdown was a conservative 60 percent bonds, and 40 percent stocks.

We also looked at her last statement and found that her current broker had been trading her portfolio very aggressively. Besides the excessive commissions, the tax consequences on short-term profits were tremendous.

Anna understood none of this. She didn't even know that she had signed a piece of paper that gave her broker discretion over her account. "Why are you doing this to yourself?" I asked. "Are you afraid of handling your money?"

And so we had a long talk about Anna's responsibility. It had never occurred to her to question her broker, who intimidated her. "Let's start again," I said. "If you want to work with us, let's work together to make sense out of your money.

"And think about a career planner for Scott!" I added.

◆ ◆ ◆

The training program now required six weeks of schooling in New York City. I begged Brad not to make me go. Stacey had been through enough changes already, including switching schools as a senior. "I can't leave my kid," I said.

Brad backed me up, and although the training director was furious, I stayed in Los Angeles. Such reasonable and considerate behavior was a pleasant surprise.

But soon Brad had disconcerting news; he was moving on and recommended that I leave this branch, too. "Go to the Beverly Hills office," he said. "You'll do more business, and anyway, I won't be here to watch over you much longer."

So I packed up my things and moved to Beverly Hills, where I was the only woman broker among twenty-eight men. Still, my manager immediately understood that I was a potential gold mine: People liked me, I was honest, and clients were already giving me their money to invest.

I didn't know much about Drexel, and I had never heard of Mike Milken, who was the firm's star. Drexel was simply an investment bank and brokerage firm, like Merrill Lynch, but not nearly as large. It did become more famous, though, because of its unusual junk-bond business.

Initially the junk-bond business meant buying **fallen angels,** or bonds that were once high grade but had slipped from grace. Milken analyzed these companies carefully and invested in those he thought were still potentially viable, and discovered that he could make a great deal of money. But Milken took the idea to a new level, realizing he could create new, higher-yielding bonds and finance companies that were not considered investment grade.

At the time I didn't know a bond from a halo. So I turned myself into a learning sponge, trying to soak up every piece of information possible. It was a constant and excellent education.

If it hadn't been for my rich friend offering me his account, I might not have gotten off to such a good start. But even with that account as a solid base, I worked as hard as anyone ever could.

I had several factors working in my favor.

One was that I was perfectly willing to admit, whenever I became baffled by events, that I still knew little about what I was doing. I had no ego. So what if I looked like a novice? I *was* a novice. Why bother to pretend anything else?

I always tried to bring some humanity to my job, too. I never bullied or hurt anyone. I learned as much about my clients as I could, and my behavior with each and every one was the same. They were all stars to me, whether their account was $5,000 or $500,000—it didn't matter, because I was grateful to anyone willing to trust me with her money.

Also, I never let the fact that I was working with a bunch of 23-year-old boys bother me. Actually, I liked being different, and once they realized I didn't have any attitude, we had fun together. Best of all, I learned from those boys. I watched them cold-call thousands of people, and I saw how things were done at the beginning level. Not that I myself could quite cold-call—instead, I did what I called warm-calling: making a list of everyone I knew, however slightly, and calling to say that I was working at a bond house, and that interest rates were high, which made bonds a good buy, so why not buy them, and why not from me?

Furthermore, I never pitched anything I didn't understand. I wasn't saying to people, "Come with me, I'm the best in the business, I know these bonds inside and out." When something new came up that I didn't understand, I'd tell my client that I needed to get someone else's input, and I'd go get it. I never lied about my knowledge. My clients learned as I learned. I sought out information about bonds as though they were the Holy Grail, which, in a way, they were for me.

And I worked as hard as I could. If that meant losing my social life, that was okay. If it meant not going on dates, that was okay, too. No one hands you a good job on a silver platter. You have to make the job work for you, and I did everything I could to succeed.

But I never skimped on my time with my daughters. In fact, in some ways they were the key to my success, because I wanted them to have everything: college, beautiful weddings, nice things. When I won the 1994 award for Los Angeles–area Entrepreneur of the Year in financial services, I went up on stage, and after every man who won an award thanked his business partners and his wife for giving him motivation, I thanked my business partner and my daughters. I said, "I want to thank my children for giving me a reason to work." People laughed, but it was the simple truth.

The bottom line was that I promised to give every one of my clients my fullest attention and care. Perhaps someone else could offer them twenty years of experience, but I offered excellent, caring, straightforward service, and people responded to that.

And despite how cynical the world can seem, there are some nice people out there. Many people responded to my pitch not because they needed my services but because they were kind enough to admire what I was trying to do. "She used to live like an heiress," they said, "and now look at her." They didn't have to hire me, but they did, and I showed my gratitude by working so hard for them.

Not that there wasn't plenty of adversity. One day I was walking around the office, meeting people and digging up information, when a man introduced himself and showed me some material about a preferred stock he wanted me to sell.

"I'll look into the company," I said, "and have someone help me do the research."

"Lady," he snarled, "you aren't in research. You're in sales. Don't you get it?"

I walked away in complete shock. He meant, Don't figure it out. Just sell it.

At this point it hadn't yet occurred to me that I was only a salesperson, and I panicked. I had thought of myself as something much more, like an investment adviser. A salesperson? It seemed wrong to me. Then I realized, I could make my own way, no matter what the rules. A closed door doesn't mean that it can't be opened. So I learned how to find access to the analysts.

Of course, I made some mistakes along the way. I listened to, and acted on, some self-serving advice from others, assuming that they knew more than I did because they were senior people. They often didn't. The worst mistake I made was being sweet-talked by some real showmen who turned up at my office with so many bells and whistles that I fell for their presentation, even though the product they were selling was mini steel mills, which were no more familiar to me than Minnie Mouse. Those mini mills went nowhere, and cost me a great client. But I gained a valuable lesson: Don't buy into something you don't understand.

The day after I lost that client, my biggest customers appeared. Instead of asking about my credentials, they wanted to know who I was, how I thought, and what made me tick. They were looking for integrity. I never sold myself as a genius, but as an honest person. And that's what they wanted for their $15 million account, which I landed.

When my first year ended, I looked at my earnings and nearly cried. My goal had been to make $40,000. I had made $106,000! Now it was like being Mildred Pierce after her restaurant had taken off. I bought a condo from a bankrupt real-estate developer and treated myself to some nice work clothes.

My career continued to grow, and by working so hard and staying so focused, I turned into one of the most successful brokers at Drexel. I was made a vice president, then a senior vice president. I had become a hot commodity for Drexel.

◆ ◆ ◆

Right after the stock market crash of 1987, a broker called me from Florida to say that he wanted to buy junk bonds, but no one at Drexel would sell to him, because he only wanted fifty. So I completed his transaction, after which he said, "I've never broken through your trading desk before."

A light bulb went off: Why didn't Drexel sell to these guys? It turned out that the big traders didn't want to be bothered with the small customers, but I decided that these customers could be a gold mine for me, so I called dozens of small firms and asked if they'd be interested in Drexel Burnham research if I could get them bonds.

"Yes," they all replied.

So there I was, creating this lucrative little institutional business without telling a soul, including my manager. I just took the orders and made the money.

A few months later I received a call from a trader upstairs, asking what I was doing. "Not much," I said, "just selling these bonds to small brokerage firms."

The trader then gave me instructions on how to sell, for his department wanted to control my activity. Meanwhile, my boss was discouraging me, because he didn't want me to be out of his control, either. I didn't like this new turn of events, so I decided to talk to Mike Milken himself.

I practiced my speech over and over until I was prepared, and then called him up.

"Who are you?" his secretary asked. After I explained, she said, "We'll get back to you."

But she didn't. So I called again, and I asked others to tell Milken about me.

Meanwhile, fate reared its unpleasant little head again.

My new condominium was a delight—pretty, quiet, and maintenance-free. It didn't have a garden, but it was large enough for me and both kids, because Audrey was now staying with me prior to her marriage.

One rainy late-winter night, while Stacey was staying at a friend's house, I was awoken by someone banging on my front door. Something smelled peculiar, but I couldn't quite place it. Then the woman from across the hall began screaming a garbled story about a burning candle, a flaming couch, and a catastrophe. When Audrey and I opened the door, since our windows were also open, billowing black smoke flew straight in, blinding us.

We were terrified. The condo across the hall was in flames, and in a short time ours would be, too.

The smoke was so thick we couldn't see, and so we held hands, crawling along the walls until, in the confusion, we became separated in the hallway. I started screaming.

A strange man eventually pulled me down the stairs. I was covered in soot. But they couldn't find Audrey. "She's not up there," they said. "We can't find her."

The building was dripping with flames, and for a full half-hour I was convinced that my baby had died, and I was inconsolable. But finally a fireman carried Audrey outside. It turned out she had bumped into a hysterical elderly woman who needed help, so Audrey went into her condo and stuffed towels under her door. She then called the fire department—no one else had done so yet. "You have to come get me," she said calmly. "I'm getting married soon and I can't die."

I've always felt that if Audrey ran this country, everything would work much more efficiently.

The condo was a complete and total wreck. Without a place to sleep, Audrey and I had to check into a hotel, and although all my belongings were reduced to a soot-covered bathrobe and my purse—

not even a single pair of underwear was left—I had to go to work the next day.

But having learned my lesson about insurance, I'd already purchased replacement-cost insurance. So the disaster that could have been, wasn't.

◆ ◆ ◆

The next day, Mike Milken's assistant called. "Come on up," she said.

I was wearing my only dress, which I'd bought that morning.

Milken gave me twenty minutes, all the while staring at me with head cocked, eyes alert, while I tried to sell him my new sales concept. When I finished, he said, "It's a good idea."

"Is that it?" I asked. "Do you want to hear more? Can I do it? When can I start?"

"Let me think about it," he said.

A few days later the head of trading called me up for another interview and I realized the job was mine. The man, who was as tough and mean-spirited as he was brilliant, simply said, "We're going to hire you. What have you been making?"

When I told him, he replied, "We'll pay you that as a base salary, and you can make twice that as a bonus."

I was so proud of myself. I had learned another huge lesson, which was how to jump on an opportunity. The call from that salesman in Florida had reached me through a fluke, but once I saw how I could take advantage of the situation, I did.

Very few people had made the move from retail sales to the institutional side. My sales manager, furious because I'd been making a great deal of money for him, tried to stop me, but it was too late.

I took Heather, my assistant, with me and taught her how to sell. She turned out to be an excellent learner, and the two of us worked hard and made a good deal of money. It was a tough new world on the institutional side. Some of these guys were nice, but many were disgusting and intentionally mean, talking to new arrivals like dirt.

"Do this, do that, screw you," they'd say. The first year was like a college frat hazing.

I didn't care—I'd been through too much to let this bother me, and instead I just quietly took advantage of all the knowledge to build a solid business. The work was exhausting. I used to wake up in the middle of the night and take a shower with a coffee cup under my chin because it was so ugly to be up at 3:45 A.M. But I had to be at work at 4:45 A.M., for the first research meeting at 5:00 A.M. And since Milken himself took 3:00 A.M. meetings, you couldn't complain— aloud, at least. I ate dinner at 4:30 P.M. and went to bed at 8:00 P.M. I gained huge amounts of weight because I was eating all day. All we did was work, eat, and sleep, and then work more, eat more, and, if we were lucky, sleep. Several times I dozed off at my desk.

Most important, for the first time in my life, I decided I could do without men. After the fire I bought a new condo with the insurance money. "I don't want to stop seeing you," I told John, "but I'm in a new phase. I want to move by myself."

There! I'd said it. Living alone, having a man at my convenience instead of at his: This was new territory to me, just as new as having a job and taking good care of myself. The very idea that a woman could exist in this world without a man, and exist happily, had always struck me as a novel concept. I knew that other women had done it, but I never believed that they could be truly happy. Even less, that they were safe. What if a disaster occurred? Who would take care of them?

But enough calamities had come along in my life to make me realize I was a survivor, with or without anyone else. At the end of the day, it was all up to me.

This isn't to say I don't think men can be great. I do, very much so. It's just that I finally made that wonderful transition from needing men to enjoying them.

John was a good friend, and he was there for me. But life had changed. That inordinately long chapter of my life, the one filled with catastrophe, suffering, and death, had ended. I'd made it. Now I wanted to live alone. Over the next few months John and I saw each other often, and we always had fun, but the relationship faded. I wasn't needy anymore. I felt secure. And John, too, felt the change. When we met, our situations were relatively equal. Now John and I were in different worlds.

Although I was making money, I was also smart enough to know that just making money wasn't enough: I had to plan for what would happen the day that I stopped making it.

Retirement

My friend Carol has a lovely 20-year-old daughter named Ashley, while Carol herself is only 42. Carol married her high-school sweetheart right out of college, and the couple is not only still together, but deeply in love after all these years. The two of them have a wonderful relationship: warm, caring, communicative.

Carol recently asked me to have a talk with Ashley who, her mother fears, has developed some irresponsible attitudes. Carol's husband has done well in real estate, and Carol suspects that Ashley doesn't understand the value of money. However, Carol claims that she herself has worked hard to remain informed about her husband's finances and cognizant of all other money matters.

"Give her one of those rousing talks of yours," Carol said. "Make sure she's aware of all the issues money brings, from her first job all the way to retirement."

I promised to do whatever I could, and then I asked Carol, as long as she'd brought it up, how *she* was planning for her own retirement. She seemed surprised, and then looked hurt.

"I'm just forty-two, remember?" she said.

I sighed, and then patted the sofa next to me. "Why don't you sit down," I said. "Before I meet Ashley, I think we need to have a little chat."

I don't know why it's so, but getting women—even well-educated, highly responsible women such as Carol—to think about retirement can be difficult.

The reality is that women are in much worse shape than men when it comes to retirement. According to recent Department of Labor statistics, three out of five women who work in the private sector don't have a pension plan. Furthermore, women have less discretionary income available for savings than men, since they earn 72¢ for every $1.00 a man makes. And, women change jobs more than men do—every 5.8 years, versus 7.6 for men—meaning that they're less likely to become vested in company pension plans. As of now, 55 percent of men over the age of 55 receive some pension benefits, but only 32 percent of women do.

Part of the problem is that people don't want to think about aging, particularly in a country like ours with its emphasis on youth. They'd rather pretend they'll never grow old. No wonder *Peter Pan* was such a success. And anyway, the whole concept of old age itself seems too abstract. It'll never happen, you think when you're 20. Then, one day, you wake up and you're there.

A lot of women fear aging—and so do many men, for that matter. But the truth is, like it or not, 65 is in your future, if you're not there already. All the dieting and liposuction in the world isn't going to change that.

For some women, it isn't just fear of aging that concerns them. At our seminars we ask participants to list their greatest worries, and over and over we hear the same refrain. "I don't want to be a bag lady in thirty years." "I'm afraid I'll be old and have nothing left." "I don't want to be on the street when I'm sixty-five." As far as I can tell from these responses, the ultimate fear isn't just being old, but being old without the resources to take care of yourself.

This one-two combination of age and helplessness so overwhelms many women that they often become afraid to take the steps necessary to prepare for life's post-working phase. On the one hand, they don't want to deal with the issue. And, they also don't want to deal with what dealing with the issue entails—sacrifice. Sacrificing that beautiful car, or that fabulous house, or that wonderful vacation that you don't need today, in order to add to your retirement savings plan for tomorrow.

Everything in life is a trade-off, isn't it? Today, you're earning $100,000 a year, which means that after taxes you've got about $65,000, and you really need only $55,000 to live, which means that you could save $10,000 this year, but instead you desperately want that beautiful new camper so that you and your husband can take terrific summer vacations, and one day on an impulse you go ahead and buy the camper. Well, there go your retirement savings. Perhaps you'll have to live in that camper when you reach 65.

Or maybe you want to buy that fabulous modern house, or that new designer original. Sure, you can buy these things now, but when you do, you're hurting your golden years. Every choice you make now affects your retirement later. The person who retires well is always sacrificing today for tomorrow.

People don't like that. It goes against one of the pillars of American society: instant gratification. "I have money now," people say to me, "and I want things now. What's the use of having money if you lock it up in some account someplace and can't touch it until you're sixty?"

I don't say that you can't spend some of your money. Of course you can. I love spending money. Most people do. Buy that new dress. Just don't buy two. Take that vacation. But don't go first class. Spend wisely, and remember that the more money you put away today, the more you'll have in ten, twenty, or thirty years.

◆ ◆ ◆

Several other issues come up at our seminars. One that I find particularly worrisome is the kind of thinking that goes: "I don't have to worry about my future. Something will turn up."

When I dig further, the woman often admits that this "something" is actually a "someone"—or, more bluntly, a man. A man who's going to step up to the plate and take care of her. A man who's going to ensure that her old age is comfortable.

Some women start this fantasy young, and they never let go. When they're 60, they're still talking about that great guy who's going to rescue them. And then retirement suddenly confronts them, and they get the short end of the stick. Why not base your plans on reality instead of fantasy? Reality is much more likely to happen.

Sure, it would be nice if someone came along to take care of you. And it happens, now and then. But should you count on it? Absolutely not.

Another issue concerning retirement is the changing rate of life expectancy. Once upon a time living to the age of 65 was considered a long life span—both my parents were dead at 60. But these days you have to consider that you'll probably live well beyond 65. Many people have relatives in their nineties. And considering all the attention our generation is giving to low-fat diets and exercise programs, some of us will live into our hundreds—a woman's life expectancy is already almost 80. So even if all your relatives died before retirement age, it doesn't mean that you shouldn't be thinking seriously about living past 70. Yes, there is evidence that our life spans are determined in part by our genes, and if your parents died at relatively young ages, you may be more likely to do the same than someone whose parents lived to be 100. But environment plays an important role too, and many of the diseases that killed off our ancestors are now controllable, or even curable, with modern medicine.

Plan your life as though it's going to be a long one. Do you want your money to run out at 71, while you make it to 96?

Yet a different problem for many women is that, while most young men have grown up familiar with the notion of retirement, women haven't been in the workplace long enough to establish female-retirement role models. We're only now seeing the first full generation of women in the workforce. Men have witnessed legions of fathers who've worked for forty-five years and then retired at 65 with a gold watch and a pension. Do you know many women who have spent a lifetime at IBM? There are some, but compared to those of men, their numbers are small.

And still one more point: Because women have had to battle through the last couple of decades for jobs and equal pay with men, much of our fighting energy has gone into establishing a solid career, rather than planning to end one. Progress takes place one step at a time: left foot, right foot, one after the other. Step one was the realization that we had to work, step two was getting a damned job, step three was getting a decent damned job, and then came step four: trying to get equal pay for that same damned job that the man next to you was earning more money for doing. The next step is obvious: learning what to do with the money you now control.

◆ ◆ ◆

When planning how much money you need for retirement, the most important question to consider is, what does the term mean for you? Over the years this image will change: Retirement, to an 18-year-old, looks different than it does to someone who's 58.

To me, retirement means that you can stop working for a living and do what you actually want to do. You can enjoy the rest of your years in the style to which you've become accustomed. That last phrase is what most people forget. What life-style do you want? Retirement means more than not working anymore. It means living well, while not working.

I find that the women accustomed to living on a budget generally plan their retirement best. For instance, a teacher with a simple life-style and low salary, whose retirement is funded through a basic employee pension program, is securing for herself a plan that won't drastically change her life. She already knows how to live within her means and can switch over to her pension painlessly. The more complicated problems arise with women who currently make a great deal of money and who haven't instituted any plans for retirement. Someone who's been making $100,000 a year may have a much harder time living on less—and yet she's also less likely to have saved the equivalent amount of her income. For instance, if a 40-year-old woman, spending $100,000 a year, wants to live in the same manner when she's 65, and assuming that inflation averages 3 percent a year for the next 25 years, she'll need to have more than $2,615,000 sitting in investments, giving her a rate of return of 8 percent a year. If her investments pay her 5 percent, and inflation averages 5 percent, she'll need more than $6,775,000 to maintain her current life-style.

When calculating how much money you will need for retirement, figure out what your current needs are—how much you spend, where you spend it—and then project that into the future by factoring in inflation.

And please, for those of you who aren't earning a living, but have come into a lump sum: Yes, you're very lucky, but that doesn't mean you can go out and spend it all before you hit 65. You must preserve your money so you can live well the rest of your life. Gear your spending now toward how much you want on hand later.

◆ ◆ ◆

Here's something of consequence to keep in mind when thinking about these figures: You're never too young to start saving. Never.

There are two fundamental truths about a retirement savings program. The first is that nothing leads to better investment results than time. A thousand dollars, put aside in a tax-free account for twenty years at 10 percent interest, will grow to $6,727. In forty years, it will be $45,259. And if you're able to hold it for sixty years, you'll have accumulated more than $300,000 on that original $1,000. (Think that can't happen? Some people are lucky enough to have grandparents who give them money when they're born. Or maybe you were a child model. Who's going to argue with a rich 3-year-old?) The point is, over time, nothing beats time. It's the best friend an investor ever had.

Let's say you have two options. One is to invest $75 every month at an average rate of 8.5 percent a year. The other is to wait ten years, and then invest $187.50 a month—or 2.5 times $75—also at 8.5 percent. At the end of twenty years, which plan will give you more money? In the first, you've invested only $18,000, and in the second, you've put in $22,500, but the first plan will net you more than $47,000, while the second plan will give you just over $35,000. That's a difference of approximately $12,000, just by giving your money more time to grow.

The way money grows is by **compounding,** which refers to the way interest is earned on the principal amount, and is then reinvested. Every time interest is earned, it's added to the principal, so the base amount grows. Earning interest on an ever-greater amount accelerates the money's growth.

The second fundamental of savings is **discipline.** Saving doesn't come easily to most people. But the sooner you learn how to do it, the better off you'll be. A regular amount of money paid to yourself every month is the surest way to guarantee a savings account. Save money each and every month. Pay yourself X percent of your salary. Then, at the end of the month, if you have money left over, put that into your investment portfolio, too.

The discipline that forces you to save a certain amount of money each month comes in handy in another arena. Remember that time is your friend—and you should never betray a friend. And how would you do that? By forgetting that saving for retirement is a long-term investment. You need the discipline to stay put with that money. Even if your IRA has tripled in the last few years, avoid the temptation to withdraw your funds. The moment you do, that money will be taxed at ordinary income rates, and you'll be fined an extra 10 percent to boot. And why take money out of something that's otherwise tax-free, anyway?

I'm not saying you can never splurge. But be prudent when you do, or you may not have anything left when you're 65.

◆ ◆ ◆

Speaking of not being able to count on treats, you can't depend on Social Security, either. Estimates vary as to how long this government agency will remain solvent, but the betting is that it won't be long. And even if the money doesn't run out, or if the government finds a way to reform the agency, Social Security doesn't offer a full retirement program—its benefits are too low, with a maximum payment of about $1,500 a month. When the system was designed, Social Security paid small but reasonable benefits. Inflation has taken care of that over the years.

In place of Social Security have evolved all the other retirement-savings plans you've heard about: the 401(k), the 403(b), pensions, IRAs (individual retirement accounts), Keoghs, SEPs (simplified employee pension plans), etc. All of these plans offer you ways to grow your money tax-deferred. Any time the government offers you such an opportunity, jump on it. Such chances are unlikely to come around often.

A **401(k)** is a plan that allows you to put aside a portion of your pretax salary and place it into a retirement account where it will grow tax-free. Thus your overall taxable income is reduced by the amount you contribute, plus you get the tax-free savings, and on top of that, many employers will match your contributions. You may invest this money as you see fit, but with some exceptions, you can't withdraw money without penalties before you reach age $59^1/2$. You can lend yourself part of the money whenever you wish, however. There are other rules and considerations to keep in mind, so study your plan well.

A **403(b)** is for those who work for charitable or other not-for-profit organizations. It's similar to a 401(k), but contains enough differences to require some careful analysis if you qualify for one.

If you're self-employed, or employed but not part of a company retirement plan (or your yearly income is below a certain cutoff), you can set aside money for retirement by placing pretax dollars into a tax-deductible **IRA** (individual retirement account); for instance, if you make $50,000 a year, and you put aside $2,000 (the maximum contribution for a single person), and have no other deductions, you'd be taxed on $48,000 income. Even if you're employed and don't qualify for tax-deductible contributions, you can still put aside the money in an IRA and earn tax-free interest. An IRA can't be withdrawn until you reach age $59^1/2$ without resulting in a 10 percent penalty, plus your normal tax rate (although there are, as always, a few exceptions).

The 1997 tax bill changed some of the rules concerning IRAs, with new penalty-free withdrawals for college tuition and first-time home purchases. Other changes included contributions for nonworking spouses of individuals with pension funds. Your tax adviser can help you sort out how the new tax bill might affect you.

A **Keogh** is a retirement plan that anyone with self-employed income can set up. As with an IRA, the earnings on your savings aren't taxable, and the contribution is also tax-deductible. Also as with other plans, you can't touch the money until you're $59^1/2$. There are several kinds of Keoghs, but all allow you to contribute more than is allowable for an IRA plan. There are also careful formulas telling you what portion of your income can be contributed, so once again, study the plan carefully before taking action.

A **simplified employee pension plan** (SEP) is also tailor-made for anyone who has some self-employment income. A SEP is deposited directly into your IRA accounts and again, specific formulas dictate how much you can contribute, and when.

Pension plans, the most traditional form of corporate retirement plans, vary widely from company to company, but there are two basic types: defined benefit plans, in which the amount you receive when you retire is determined in advance, and defined contribution plans, in which you don't know how much you'll have to retire on until you retire. You should check with your employer to see which type, if either, you have, and save according to the rules. Pension plans work best for those who stay put at one company, since most plans require that you work a certain number of years before you're vested—or are part of the plan.

The IRS has a hot line for anyone interested in these plans: (800) 829-3676. You can also call the American Association of Retired Persons (AARP): (202) 434-2277.

There are other issues to consider when planning retirement, and primary among these is **health insurance.** While government Medicare covers everyone over the age of 65, Medicare is to health what Social Security is to income—it pays a minimum amount. If it's all you can afford, then you learn to make it work. But one reason to save more money from your twenties to your sixties is to make sure that, when you're aging, you have the best available coverage. You want to have all possible choices in medical care.

Once you pass retirement age, if you've been working for a company, you'll also have to consider replacing company-sponsored group health plans. Very often these plans are less expensive, or offer more daily care, or more office visits, than programs such as Blue Cross and Blue Shield or other plans you buy on your own—so, after you leave the company plan, your payments will increase, and this needs to be factored into your living expenses.

One way you can save a little money is by starting these programs early. When you turn 50, the magazine *Modern Maturity* appears in your mailbox, like it or not—and believe me, many women don't want to be reminded. In the magazine (a publication of the AARP) you'll see various ideas concerning your choices beyond Medicare, including COBRA (Consolidated Omnibus Budget Reconciliation Act of 1985), which in certain circumstances extends company health coverage, and Medigap insurance, which covers the gaps in Medicare. Take them seriously. Similarly, as we discussed in the insurance section, investigate long-term care insurance policies as well.

◆ ◆ ◆

When I talk about retirement, still one more subject frequently arises. In fact, the more seminars we hold, the more often we run into this predicament: It's not just your own retirement you need to consider. For many of you in what we're now calling the sandwich generation, retirement planning concerns your parents, too. Not all of them have taken care of themselves as well as we're recommending that you do.

For instance, Jack, the 30-year-old son of a close friend, is already helping his mother face her retirement. She earns $45,000 a year, but she never planned ahead; worse, her husband died two years ago from cancer, leaving no life insurance. Of course, he hadn't expected to die, but then, few of us at age 58 do. Jack's mother has some cash flow, but she can't afford to live in her condominium anymore. In fact, she had to walk away from it, because she couldn't sell it for enough money to pay off her mortgage.

Today Jack and his wife are planning ahead to make sure that Jack's mother has something to live on besides her Social Security, so that she never has to walk away from an obligation again. It's an expense they hadn't counted on, but it's one they can't avoid. This is an issue we'll be seeing more frequently: structured plans for your parents as well as for you and your kids.

Chapter 10

Success, and Five Important Rules

Just about the time you think you can make both ends meet, somebody moves the ends.

Pansy Penner

I remained at Drexel for a little over two more years, selling a few hundred million dollars' worth of bonds. And because I wanted to build a team of competent, intelligent, qualified women, I hired two other women to work with me.

But Drexel's high-yield department was undergoing a criminal investigation by the U.S. Attorney's office, as well as the Securities and Exchange Commission, based on allegations of insider trading and other charges. Mike Milken had been removed. The other men were, at best, difficult. Once I went into a meeting with some traders a day after I'd been absent with the flu. "Sick?" one asked. "That's not an excuse unless you had your goddamned head stuck in a toilet." The men snickered.

That was one of the nicer exchanges. Once a trader threw a heavy metal disk at another trader, nearly ripping his eye out. Another man tore the necktie off a manager's neck during an argument. I could deal with most of these rude indignities, but the one that sent me hurtling out of Drexel for good took place the day one of the major traders came to me and said, "I want you to sell Eastern Airline Third Equipment Trust."

These were the third mortgage on a group of airplanes; the first mortgage was a very solid investment, but as I told this bond trader,

171

the second was very risky, and a third, well . . . "I definitely don't think these bonds are appropriate for my customers," I replied.

"You're not paid to think," he snapped back.

"I'm not going to take this from you," I said.

"Yeah?" He looked ugly. "What are you going to do about it?"

I strode away and found my coworker, Neil, next to whom I'd been working for some time and had come to admire. "I'm resigning," I told him. "I've had it here. I'm walking out now."

"Slow down," Neil said. Then he surprised me. "Maybe I'll go with you."

The investigation into Drexel had been gaining ground. Because it didn't impact my work I'd paid little attention, but Neil was captivated by it all and he bet that the whole place was going to go down. He turned out to be quite right. Mike Milken, indicted in March 1989 on ninety-eight counts, including securities fraud and related crimes, pleaded guilty to six felonies on November 21, 1990, and was sentenced to ten years in prison and fines of $650 million. In February 1990, Drexel filed for bankruptcy protection.

Once Mike Milken had been removed from Drexel, there was no reason for me to stay. No matter what anyone thinks of Mike Milken, he *was* Drexel, from start to finish. He made it a remarkable place for me and everyone else who worked in his department. And few others would have given me that interview or hired me for the job. Despite all that happened to him, it's hard for me not to feel grateful to him.

"Then let's go out together as a team," I told Neil. "Very few people have ever left this department before. We could write our own ticket."

I immediately set up some preliminary interviews and we went to New York, Neil representing the investment research side, while I was the trading and relationship person.

The last time I'd gone out on interviews, no one wanted me. What a difference six years can make. Now everyone was interested. Before, they wouldn't let me take their test. Now Merrill Lynch was offering us a huge signing bonus.

But all this made me wonder: If these firms were willing to pay us so much money, what were we *really* worth? Furthermore, I was tired of having people tell me what to do. So we decided to set up our own shop.

I went to my department manager at Drexel and told him I was leaving. "But let us go nicely," I said. "We'd like to be able to buy bonds from you. We'll be one of your best customers."

My boss thanked me for the honesty, and he allowed us to stay as long as necessary.

Neil's patience had been appropriate. As much as I wanted to, we couldn't just set ourselves up the next day. It took time: We had to take tests, get licenses, find an office, buy furniture, and raise money.

Eventually I called two women bankers I knew in Newport Beach. Someone smart once told me that I should put my money in a bank where I could build a good relationship, rather than the one that paid an extra fraction of a percent in interest rates. I always try to listen to smart people, so I took his advice. It takes only a few minutes to talk to others. And since I'm such a full-disclosure person, others tend to be candid with me. The result was that these two bankers and I ended up helping one another's careers. Even when I moved to Los Angeles I continued working with them, so when it came time to apply for a loan, they knew I always paid my bills and they knew my credit history.

Neil had completed excellent spreadsheets, and although we didn't have a business plan, our projections were solid. (In fact, after the first year, we were almost right on the nickel.)

We set up the brokerage business we called Dabney Resnick in July 1989.

Our investment banking department happened almost by accident. In late fall 1989, a close friend from my Drexel days approached me and said that Milken had hired three smart young bankers for his new group, and then realized he wasn't going to be allowed in that business —so perhaps we should hire them. I went to Neil and said, "This offer has some big advantages for us. They'll pay for themselves, and maybe this will put us in the deal business." Neil agreed, and they came aboard.

About six months after our company started, Drexel went out of business, and it seemed as if half its former employees approached us about a job. Seeing a great opportunity, we hired some salespeople and, trying to remain open to new ideas, we also hired some excellent research people. We grew much more quickly than I would have thought possible.

This wasn't quite where I wanted to be—I was more interested in managing money—but, as they say, you can't fight the tape. The firm seemed to have its own momentum. We began to expand, building on our strength in niche markets. As we grew our institutional business, we added other components until we emerged as a full-service investment bank and brokerage firm.

It hasn't always been easy. There have been some hard times and, as in any business, I've discovered things and people that weren't to my liking. For instance, in 1994 I hired my lawyer to become my chief operating officer, because I didn't enjoy the day-to-day management of the brokerage firm, and he soon discovered several staff problems. I had to learn that simply because I cared for someone personally didn't mean he or she was right for the position.

In late 1996 Dabney/Resnick formed a strategic alliance with Imperial Credit Industries Inc., a publicly traded, diversified financial-services company; in so doing, we changed the name of the company to Dabney/Resnick/Imperial.

I gave up management responsibilities, remained as chairman, and turned most of my attention to The Resnick Group, which was established in 1996. Through this company's businesses and seminars I've been able to meet thousands of women, all of whom are asking the same questions I once did. How can I make it on my own? Can I really do it without a boyfriend, or a spouse, or a partner? How can I possibly succeed in a world that I don't really understand? The only problem with meeting so many women is that there's too little time to talk about individual cases, and the particular issues that confront these attendees.

However, over the years I've found that much of my advice can be summarized in these five important rules:

1. Always be knowledgeable.

So many women tell me they'd like to know more about their family finances, but their husbands won't tell them a thing.

I say, ask. Ask him so you know.

Young women tell me their fathers won't talk to them either. Always the same answer: Ask. Ask. Ask. You must learn to ask questions. No one's going to take the time to force you to learn about your own finances. You have to make it happen. Demand it. Don't be left in the dark. When my father died, we were sure that millions were coming our way. It never occurred to us to ask him before he died about insurance, or even the state of our basic finances. We paid for it dearly. Please don't make the same mistakes. Don't bury your head in the sand.

Recently Margot, a schoolteacher and recent widow, came to my office to talk. While her husband Bill was alive her family had lived nicely: They owned a large house and their children attended private schools. Margot assumed that the family finances were excellent. But after Bill died of a heart attack, Margot discovered that, in order to live so well, Bill had exhausted the couple's savings account, built up debt, and had allowed the premiums on his life insurance to lapse so he could pay for the children's private schools. The morning after Bill's death, Margot woke up destitute. The only way she was able to survive financially was by selling her house and allowing her friends to set up a fund to keep her afloat. Margot told me she was furious at Bill, but I told her that being angry wasn't going to do any good, since Bill was dead, and anyway, it was Margot who never bothered to understand the couple's finances.

How do you go about asking your husband about money? Just as you would discuss anything else that affects the two of you. You must be open, you must sit down and talk. Sure, some husbands may feel you're invading their territory. There's no need to get a divorce over this. Just explain that you need to feel knowledgeable. Who knows? He may be thrilled at your interest. But don't ask for the moon the first time. Begin at the beginning. Tell your husband that you want to share financial statements, that you'd like to meet with the broker or money manager once or twice a year, and that you'd like to participate in your estate and tax planning. It's like any other form of decision making, such as choosing where you're going to live, or what car you're going to buy. Carry out the financial part of your marriage similarly. Make it communal. You can't blame your husband if you say, "Don't make me learn this," and then something happens to him, leaving you at the world's mercy. You're part of the formula.

You don't need to know a lot. You just need to understand your investments, your insurance, and your financial plans. From there proceed at your own pace. But by all means proceed.

2. Understand what you sign.

Back in the 1970s, when my father asked me to sign a few pieces of paper, how was I to know that I was giving away the deed to my own house? It never occurred to me that I could actually read the document he threw in front of me. Why should I? My father knew what he was doing, and I didn't. Besides, I had so many other things to think about.

I also willingly signed that option agreement that made it possible for my father's partners to buy me out of the business against my will.

For years I thought I was the only woman stupid enough to do such things. But once I started working, I ran into dozens of women who had acted similarly. I couldn't believe it! I met one woman the other day who, without knowing it, had signed over her entire brokerage account to her husband. He wasn't trying to cheat her. He was simply a control freak and didn't like the idea that his wife had holdings he couldn't manipulate.

No one's perfect. But signing away your money without so much as a simple question makes no sense.

Do you look at the papers you sign? When your husband, or your broker, or your accountant, gives you a sheaf of papers, do you read them? Don't be a financial illiterate. Learn to read before you sign.

3. Protect yourself.

Here's another story that I've heard more than once, and it's one that makes me sad. It concerns Faith, a 62-year-old advertising executive, but it could have been so many others. After a solid professional career, Faith had accumulated about $300,000 in savings. Life was going swimmingly: Her two daughters had good careers, and she had five healthy, happy grandchildren. As Faith approached her retirement, she began to consider other options for her savings besides the mutual fund where she had parked them for the last decade. Several of her bridge-club friends had told her they were making 15 percent on their investments, while Faith's mutual fund was averaging about 10 percent.

One day Faith got a phone call from a honey-voiced woman who told Faith about a wonderful real-estate investment possibility in Hawaii, and what extraordinary profits everyone was making. Why, she herself had already raked in $500,000 on a mere $50,000 investment. Imagine!

Well, to make a long, unhappy story a short, unhappy one, Faith was hooked, and the next thing she knew, this very clever scam artist had skipped town after fleecing Faith out of 90 percent of her savings.

You must learn to protect yourself. This means not only making sure that you save enough money, but also making sure you don't throw it away. Sound easy? Then why do so many women get it wrong? Protect yourself. Spend only what you can afford. Don't go into debt. Make yourself a nice cushion in case things go wrong. Don't trust people who guarantee you easy money. Be kind to animals. (I threw that in to see if you were paying attention.)

4. Understand that life is not always consistent—nor are you.

Up until a few years ago, every time I thought my life had reached some kind of holding pattern, it crashed. Every time I thought that my plans were safe, they were demolished.

I'm not unique. No one has control over fate. Scores of people have made a fortune and lost it, made another, and lost that one too. My mother had a favorite saying: "People plan and God laughs."

You must organize your business affairs with fate in mind.

Let's look at Teresa, a 36-year-old divorcée who came to see me with a problem. Teresa did well from her divorce settlement, receiving

$500,000. She also has about $25,000 a year from investments, and a nice home.

Because she had that small base, Teresa figured that she didn't have to worry about life. She never lacked for boyfriends, and so she figured that before that $500,000 was gone, a new husband would arrive. After all, one always had before. So Teresa had a lot of fun with her money. But things went awry. The rich guy she started dating left her after only a year, and no one else has come along. Now, five years after the divorce, the fun is gone, as is most of Teresa's capital. Teresa never gave it a thought. Why should she, she reasoned, when she had gone through her entire life without ever worrying about money?

But there's always a first time. And now Teresa's realizing it. Chicken today, feathers tomorrow.

5. Get familiar with your inner self.

This may be my most important rule, one which I call the Principle of Holistic Wealth. Finance and psychology are inextricably related. Don't let anyone tell you otherwise. You need to know who you are in order to handle your money, because the various elements of your life—physical health, finances, relationships—all connect. The person who takes care of your health is the same person who takes care of your money: you.

The best single piece of investment advice I can give to anyone—man, woman, or child—is: Know yourself.

So maybe I'm not the first person to give this piece of advice. But the reason so many others have said the same thing is because it's important and because it's true—especially in finance where, if you don't live in reality, you can easily turn into a victim. Financial planning produced on the basis of fantasies is not going to benefit anyone.

I have a friend whom I call Holly Golightly because her grasp of reality is, shall we say, a little light. Holly once had a nice nest egg, but her husband Sterling was born to spend money—he'd already gone through his own trust fund, and although Holly was aware of this, she didn't check his spending habits, even though the money he spent was now hers. The more Sterling spent, the less Holly looked. The more she let him spend, the more money Sterling figured she had. Finally Holly's money manager called with his last warning: "Devour the rest of your principal," he said, "and you won't have a cent left when you're fifty." Holly didn't listen. Her life was a fantasy. Today she's flat broke. That's a reality.

I talked to another woman recently who came in to interview me because she was looking for a new money manager. Her old one, she complained, never kept her informed of his actions. This appealed to me because, as you now know, I believe a manager and a client must maintain good communication, and we discussed that. Then, however, she mentioned her manager's name, and he turned out to be someone I respect. The next week, in fact, I met him at a conference, where he told me that his client had already explained that she was leaving him for me. "Good luck," he said. When pressed, he told me that the woman insisted she be privy to all movements in her assets, but whenever he tried to get in touch with her, she either paid him no attention, or she refused his calls. Then, every year or so, she'd complain bitterly that he hadn't consulted her. "She thinks of herself as a wise financial type," he said. "The truth is, she's terrified of responsibility." The woman played the same game with me. Now she's looking for another money manager. It will always be this way until she faces herself.

As for myself, I know I couldn't have become successful if I hadn't been able to use my therapy to build a firm psychological foundation following all those terrible valleys in my life. Once I had established that base, I acquired the emotional tools necessary to take care of my own financial needs. In other words, once I was clear about who I was, I was able to confront and meet my financial reality with intelligence.

I don't care how you do it: meditation, analysis, yoga, running, prayer, support groups, therapy—whatever works for you. But spend time with your inner self and get to know who you are. When you do, you'll know more about your habits, your needs, and your desires. You'll also have established a better line of communication with yourself. In my case, analysis was the key—once I opened up my psyche to inspection, I was able to learn what I needed in life, and then how to get it.

Monica

I mentioned Monica at the beginning of this book. Currently almost seventy, she's suffered her share of trouble, and both her marriages ended in messy divorces, the second of which gave her well over a million dollars. However, her last broker, who'd been in business only a few months, invested her money poorly—and Monica wasn't watching. Once she realized how badly she had fared, she grabbed her account and ran. She then invested it poorly by herself. Now the portfolio is worth $300,000.

Monica also owns a condo, worth another $300,000, and a small house in Malibu, which she rents out. Monica currently spends about $8,000 a month on the condo, clothing, and other costs. She's never paid much attention to money, but it's finally hit her that she's unlikely to remarry, and that she could even live another thirty years, as her own mother did.

She enjoys her current, expensive life-style, and doesn't want to make any changes.

Monica has one married, financially independent daughter. The two aren't close, and it's unlikely, except in an emergency, that the daughter would help Monica in any way.

The first thing I told Monica was that as sorry as I was that her money had been lost, it had been her responsibility to check out her broker. These words startled her.

"It's true," I said. "The guy had only been in business for a few months. Did you ask him about his background?"

She shook her head.

"You must do due diligence on anyone you want to hire," I said. "You're trusting these people with all your money. Would you let a doctor treat you without checking him out?"

We also talked about insurance and taxes, all of which were in order. "I think we can help you," I told Monica. "But we have to look at your spending."

Once Monica gave me all her financial information, we studied her cash flow. "You're spending more than ninety thousand dollars a year," I said. "But let's figure out in very broad strokes how much money you have. There's three hundred thousand dollars in equity, one thousand dollars income a month from the apartment that you rent out. This gives you twelve thousand dollars a year. So if the three hundred thousand is well invested, and we can make you as much as ten percent interest, that will earn you thirty thousand dollars. Plus the rental, that gives you forty-two thousand dollars before taxes.

"Unfortunately, that's less than half of what you spend."

Monica didn't want to hear this, but I went on. "Something's got to give," I said. "You're going through your principal too quickly. At this rate, you'll be out of cash in less than six years."

Monica was reluctant to change her life, but the only way I could see her living happily involved a major move and a major cut in her spending. "Have you ever considered living in a city with a lower cost of living?" I asked. "For instance, do you have any friends in Palm Springs?" She did—several of her friends had moved there, for similar reasons. And she admitted that she'd given the idea thought already.

If Monica's finances had been in better shape, we would have tried to find her investments that provided her with fixed income, but instead, we decided that even though she couldn't afford to take much risk, we had to put some of her money into equity. Monica could easily live another twenty years or more, and each year, if she withdrew all her interest, inflation would eat at the value of her principal. So at least 20 percent had to go into growth. We won't take high risks on this money, but we do have to make sure that her principal doesn't wither.

To draw up a plan for Monica, we ended up assuming that she sold her $300,000 house (and paid no capital gains tax, since she got close to what she paid for it) and invested most of her money. Of that, we suggested that 20 percent go into growth, divided among the Standard & Poor's 500 Index Fund, a small-cap mutual fund, and emerging market and developed country funds.

Then, 25 percent went into income and growth, into an array of convertible bond funds and preferred stocks. The other 55 percent went into income-producing investments: an assortment of high-yield bonds, bonds issued by government agencies, and other types of bonds.

In some cases we recommend a woman become involved with her

portfolio. Not here. In the past Monica had panicked too often, behaving in a knee-jerk style, selling at lows, buying at highs. She's not suited for a heavy involvement in investments. Instead, we created a plan and asked her to stick with it. Period.

I didn't tell her this, but Monica's portfolio poses a difficult problem. She should have planned her finances a long time ago, but instead she kept looking for a man to take care of her. I refrained from giving her a lecture, however. She knew what had happened to her life and she didn't need me to remind her. It was time to start anew, and for her willingness to do that, I admire her. When last I heard, she'd listed her home in Malibu and was already renting an apartment in Palm Springs. Good for her!

Chapter 11

Judy's Last Two Golden Rules

I know of nothing more despicable and pathetic than a man who
devotes all the hours of the waking day to the making of money
for money's sake.

John D. Rockefeller

*P*lease read these last two golden rules carefully. They're as important as anything else in the book—and maybe more so.

The first rule is: Never lose your integrity.

Integrity matters. Life isn't about how much money you have. Life is about being a decent, honest person. Bad acts come back to haunt you. Life really is a wheel. It's best to be moral when it comes to your money.

This doesn't mean that everyone else is going to act similarly. The world doesn't work that way. And it can be depressing to witness the kind of dishonesty that takes place in business. Dishonest people do make money. They often make more money than you ever will.

But you don't have to be immoral to do well for yourself. Do your share. Be honest. Don't break the rules.

Throughout my life I've always erred on the side of honesty. There are times when I could have made a lot more money if I hadn't. But to what end? To allow dirty money into my life? I didn't want it.

Even shading the truth is unappealing. During my stay at Drexel Burnham, management used to reward brokers with bonuses for hitting certain sales targets. One year I was $10,000 away from a bonus, so one of the bigger traders said, "I'm going to throw a trade your way so you can make up that difference." I thanked him and declined. The reward wouldn't have been real—who'd be gaining from it? The real thrill would be to hit the goal on my own. The next year, when I did make it, it was that much more pleasurable for me. I like being acknowledged for my achievements, but only when I've actually done them myself.

A lot of crooks, especially white-collar ones, get away with stealing. But that's no reason to do it. As we learned in kindergarten, it's wrong to grab things from others: "It's not nice to take Johnny's crayons," as the teacher always said. People steal because they're greedy, or lazy, and it angers me. Earn your own money. No one said it would be easy. Working hard for your money is the way to go. It feels good, and you never have to look over your shoulder.

I know one woman who disagreed with me on this subject. She embezzled a good deal of money from her husband. Why not? she thought. The marriage was miserable, but she didn't have the decency or the guts to confront her husband. Instead, she stole from her allowance money, always asking for more than she needed, and also stole cash from her husband's pocket. She made deals with local merchants—she would buy clothes at their stores, and then return them for the cash instead of the credit, giving them a small cut. Eventually she was able to siphon off more than $200,000. But during the inevitable divorce proceedings, the court discovered the money she had socked away, and it was folded into the couple's community possessions. So after all that stealing, she had to confess publicly to her thievery, and hand half of it back.

Actually, I know many women who have stolen money from their husbands. Many of them are what I call hundred-dollar-bill stashers —even my own mother occasionally pilfered hundreds, although I didn't know this until after she died. There I was, walking through her apartment, weeping and sobbing, when I felt a lump in the rug under my feet. I turned the carpet over and found, bundled in plastic wrap, a few thousand dollars in hundreds.

Stealing money gives you few options. If you were to steal $100,000, you'd save maybe $40,000 on the tax. But you couldn't invest the rest, because any time you place more than $9,000 cash into a bank account, you have to explain where it came from. Saying you found it under the rug doesn't do the trick.

But we're talking about more here than the pointlessness of having useless funds, or the fear of being caught. Being honest and ethical about your money feeds your soul. True, you may not have as much money at the end of your life than if you had cheated and lied your way through it. But what kind of a life would that have been? One of dishonesty and deceit, one filled with lies and unpleasantness. Imagine having to spend your life trying to remember which lies you told to which people. Imagine having to worry every day if the IRS was going to audit you. Imagine going to bed every night knowing that you were less than a good person. Is it worth it?

The bottom line is that no one gets away with dishonesty. I can't imagine that being a thief feels good. You're always afraid of being caught. You're always aware that you're a bad person. Who wants to go through life with that kind of a self-image? I don't. I doubt you do, either. Be honest, be fair, be kind, and make your money on the up-and-up, and the world will be a nicer place—not just for you, but for everyone around you, too.

◆ ◆ ◆

The second rule is: Always keep your perspective. Perspective matters as much as money.

In my life, I lost nearly everything that counts, and that's how I learned to prioritize. Once you lose everything, you gain perspective. It's like the myth of Pandora's box where, after all those terrible plagues and ills were released into the world, hope still lay at the bottom. No matter how bad life gets, there's always something left to hold on to.

My own hope is that you don't have to suffer. You can learn from a story like mine. By the time that fire burned down my condo, I was able to understand it was nothing—just a fire. I lost things. That's all. No one died. And I was insured. So I bought new things. I couldn't buy a new sister or a new mother.

Money can't be the center of your existence. Where would you be if you didn't have your health, your friends, your family, and your soul? Money won't buy you any of those things.

Then again, none of those things will buy money, either, and being able to afford some of the advantages money offers is important. Money is part of the formula of life. It just isn't the entire formula.

Having money has provided me with a place in life where I feel secure. Money hardly takes the place of family or health, but it is the means to a wonderful end.

Perhaps it's true, as they say, that the love of money is the root of all evil. But pay attention: It's not money itself that's bad, it's loving it. There's nothing wrong with wanting to have financial security. I certainly wanted money—not to keep it all and lord it over others, but so that I could give to the people I care for, and to the charitable causes that matter to me. Those of us who share our wealth and success get more pleasure from our money than those who hoard it. How many times in the course of civilization has this point been made? Ebenezer Scrooge learned his lesson, and so have dozens of others.

I consider myself to have been very blessed over these last few years. After all those tragedies, my life took a new, confident turn, and I'm grateful. It's true that everything I have could disappear at any moment, because nothing is forever, but as of this moment the person I have grown into can accept the money I've made and use it wisely.

Using it wisely can mean that when I make money, I give some back. It feels good to help those who aren't able to help themselves. These days my favorite causes are homeless women, especially those with children, for obvious reasons; and Crohn's disease, because my daughter Stacey suffers from it. Crohn's disease is a chronic autoimmune disease. No one knows what causes it, nor do they know how to cure it. But they do know it makes the sufferer feel completely dreadful.

I remember a time when Stacey was extremely ill, facing an uncertain future, lying in bed with an IV stuck in her chest. As a mother I felt so horribly helpless. I thought that all I'd gone through had made me invulnerable to tragedy, but there's no such immunity. Still, I had learned from experience not to be passive, so I educated myself about the disease and eventually raised hundreds of thousands of dollars for research.

My becoming proactive didn't improve my daughter's health. It didn't cure the disease. But it made me feel better. I gained some knowledge and I lost some fear. And it also made Stacey proud of me, which helps us both.

Every Christmas, I give a speech to my employees in which I remind them that all we're doing at the firm, no matter how well we do it, is making money. We're not working to cure cancer or AIDS, we're not saving starving children in Africa, we're not keeping endangered species alive. We're simply making money.

Through this speech I'm trying to reach out to the younger people with my story. I had the stuffing kicked out of me by the time I entered the world of finance. I was so grateful to earn any kind of a living at all. And every day I know something can happen that can take everything away. There could be a national disaster. My family could be hurt. Someone could undermine the success of my business and ruin me.

I get emotional during this speech. I see those 110 smiling faces, and I realize how grateful I am that my life worked out so well. When I'm finished speaking, most of my employees react warmly. Some of them come up to me afterward and say, "I heard you. I knew you were talking to me. Thank you." But there are always a few who think I'm a jerk, and I know who they are, because I'm talking about values, and those are the ones who don't have any. They don't want to hear this speech. But I make them listen anyway, and I intend to do it for the rest of my career.

◆ ◆ ◆

Money: It's not what it can buy, nor the prestige it confers, that matters. Once you see it in perspective, you understand that the greatest asset of having money is personal freedom. For me, having money means that I never have to compromise myself by living with someone I don't care for, because I'm afraid to leave him. Money means that I can take care of the other people in my life—my kids and my grandkids—the way I want to, and none of us has to depend upon someone else. Money can't buy health, but it sure helps to have it around when your family is sick so that you can pay for the doctor. But money didn't keep my family itself around.

In the business world the golden rule is often reworded: "He who has the gold, rules." To some degree, this is true. And for women, this means that once *you* have the gold, you don't have to be ruled by anyone else.

My father, who didn't mince words, once defined freedom as the ability to say "fuck you" to anyone you want. When he handed me my percentage of his business, he said, "This is your fuck-you money. That means you can say fuck you to anyone you want. You can be on your own."

His gift was an attempt to teach me the value of money and to start me on the road to independence. During the four years before he died, my father turned into my ally rather than my oppressor, and I will always be grateful for that time.

I am also grateful that his plan worked. I did become independent. I did learn the meaning of money—in every sense. Money isn't something to be worshiped. It is something to be valued. And the best way to value it is to understand it, to control it, and to own it. This is what I've learned, and I truly hope you will learn it, too.

Appendix: Life Insurance

For those of you who really are interested in knowing more about life insurance, please read on.

There are three principal reasons to buy life insurance—to replace the income lost when the principal breadwinner of a family dies; to help ease the tax burden of your estate; and as an investment.

There are, however, several different types of insurance. Before we go into them, let's define a few terms.

Life-insurance policies have **death benefits** and **premiums.**

Death benefits are the moneys paid to your designated recipient upon your death.

Premiums are the amount you agree to pay for the insurance. If you have **fixed premiums,** then you must pay your premiums every year for as long as the policy states. If you have **flexible premiums,** you pay them as often as you like, in amounts of your choice, subject to maximum and minimum amounts. And **indeterminate premiums** are premiums which can be adjusted by the insurance company, either up or down.

Some policies develop what are called **cash values.** In fact, this is the name of one of the two major types of insurance: **cash value insurance.** The other type is called **term insurance.**

In addition to paying your beneficiary or estate a benefit upon your death, a life-insurance policy may well let you accumulate money, which is its cash value, and (subject to restrictions) you're generally allowed to withdraw some of this cash.

You can also take out a loan from the insurance company, using this insurance-policy cash value as your collateral. This is called a **policy loan.**

For most policies containing cash values, that cash value grows each year at a guaranteed interest rate, which is usually pretty decent, but never spectacular.

Insurance companies are basically pessimists. They set your premium preparing for the worst: That is, they assume that they're going to earn very low interest rates and will have to pay out a lot in death benefits every year. But because interest rates are often higher than, and actual death benefits often amount to less than the company had projected, the insurance company may return some of those excess interest earnings or some of the death-benefit savings to policyholders in the form of **dividends.**

No company guarantees dividends. Furthermore, dividends rise and fall each year depending on all kinds of events that affect the insurance company, ranging from changes in the stock and bond markets to medical epidemics (i.e., the company has to pay out more money than it had anticipated).

◆ ◆ ◆

The major kinds of life insurance are called **term, whole life, universal life,** and **variable life.** (The latter three are known as **cash value.**)

A **term insurance** policy pays money, or the death benefit, if death occurs before a certain point in time, which is called the **term of the policy.** The premiums you pay usually don't increase for the term of the policy, and you may be able to renew the policy at the end of the term.

Two types of term insurance commonly sold today are **annually renewable term** and **ten-year level term** insurance. The premiums for annually renewable term increase each year, as the term of the policy is one year long.

Premiums for ten-year level term insurance increase every decade, but some companies don't allow you to renew your policy at the end of that ten-year period.

These types of term insurance are cheap, at least initially. But although the premiums start out low, since they increase every year or every ten years, it can eventually become very expensive to own them. As a result, term insurance could be right for you if you anticipate your insurance needs to last only a limited period of time, or if your income is increasing and you expect to be able to afford the higher premiums of other forms of insurance in the future.

The other forms of insurance are the more complicated ones. Still, these cash-value policies, which are initially more expensive, can save you money in the very long run.

The most common type of insurance, **whole life insurance,** comes in many forms, and its death benefit is payable when you die, or if you're lucky enough to live past 100, which the insurance company seems to equate with death. (I don't. Grandma Moses was still painting at that age. What a great time to take up a new career, especially if you've just received your million-dollar death benefit!)

The premiums for whole life can be either **fixed** or **indeterminate,** and you can pay them for as long as you live, or only up to a certain age or for a certain number of years. This latter type of policy is called a **limited payment** policy, and its premiums are generally larger than those of a policy where the premiums are paid for life.

A **participating policy** is one where you have the right to receive dividends from the company. Premiums for a participating policy are usually fixed. There are many ways that you can take these dividends, but the two most common options are to take the dividends in cash or to use them to buy additional insurance, or **paid-up additions,** which also pay dividends. So if you buy a participating life-insurance policy and use the dividends to buy additional, paid-up insurance, the death benefit can grow substantially over time. But remember that the dividends are never guaranteed.

Whole life insurance policies also have guaranteed cash values. With whole life, these values are fixed at the time you buy a policy, and won't change from what was originally promised. However, the additional paid-up insurance also has a cash value which, like the additional death benefit, can increase substantially over time.

The premiums for whole life insurance are initially much higher than the premiums for term insurance. But because the premiums are level, and the policy can pay dividends, and also because this insurance has a cash value, over time whole life can be more economical than term.

In addition, if you need cash, you can withdraw the cash value of your policy (which is called **surrendering your policy**). When you do this, you return it to the insurance company and they send you a check for any cash value which hasn't been used as collateral for a policy loan. However, you'll lose your death-benefit protection, as the policy is terminated.

You can also take a policy loan, which reduces the death benefit by the amount of the loan, but that way you still retain the rest of the death benefit.

◆ ◆ ◆

Universal life insurance is a policy with lots of flexibility. First appearing in the 1970s, these policies allow you to change the death benefit whenever you wish, and you can pay premiums as often or as infrequently as you like, and in any amount you want, subject to limitations.

Universal life insurance works like a bank account into which your premiums are added, and interest is credited by the insurance company (with certain charges deducted). Your account has a guaranteed interest rate, and if the insurance company is earning enough to pay you more, it usually will. Guaranteed charges (or expenses incurred by the insurance company) are always shown in your policy, but companies frequently charge less than these guaranteed rates. You may also run into a **surrender charge,** which reduces the amount you can withdraw from your policy. The surrender charge decreases over time, and is usually gone fifteen or twenty years after you've bought the policy.

When you're buying a universal life insurance policy, an agent will frequently provide an **illustration of values.** This is a projection into the future of both your death benefit (how much you'd get if you died, calculated each year all the way up to age 100) and your cash value (how much you'd get if you surrendered your policy) as well as the premium payments (how much you'd pay).

These illustrations are designed to show you how your cash value and death benefit will grow, and are required to show **guaranteed values** and **current or assumed values.** Guaranteed values are based on the maximum charges (the maximum amount the insurance company can withdraw from your account to pay for the cost of insurance and expenses) and the minimum interest rate they will credit to your policy. Current or assumed values are generally based on the interest rate currently credited, and the charges currently assessed by the company.

Since no one can predict the future, and illustrations project values for long periods into the future, it is unlikely that your policy cash value and death benefit will grow exactly as shown in the illustration. However, illustrations can be useful when you compare different policies from different companies. In other words, if the same premiums and death benefits are shown, the policy that has the higher cash values over time is therefore the better value.

Finally, when you buy either universal life insurance or whole life insurance, you're relying on the insurance company to make sound financial decisions. But no one is always right, and that certainly includes insurance companies. Over the last few decades several of them have made risky investments which, when they didn't pan out, caused the companies to go bust. When something like this happens, policy holders who have life insurance with cash values still have to make premium payments to pay for the insurance; the insurance companies don't disappear, so the death benefit still exists, but the companies are usually restructured, and during that time, you have only limited access to your cash value. So it's very important to find out about the financial health of a company before buying a life insurance policy from it.

Several companies rate insurance companies' financial health, including Bests, Standard & Poor's, Moody's, and Duff & Phelps. Ask your agent for these ratings. The higher the ratings, the lower the risk. (Be careful if you read these ratings without help, since each service has a different ratings key. In one system, an A + can be an excellent rating, in another it can be average. Read the keys attentively.)

◆ ◆ ◆

If any type of insurance can be called trendy, it would be **variable life.** These policies resemble universal life except that you, instead of the insurance company holding on to your money, invest it in an account. Variable accounts look like mutual funds, and are often managed by mutual-fund companies. Your cash value will rise and fall with the account you choose.

As with a mutual fund, your money can grow quickly in one of these accounts. But also similar to a mutual fund, if the value of the fund falls, you risk losses.

With variable life, since you'll usually have a choice of several funds, and you can even divide your money among these funds, you'll have more control over how your money is invested than you would in universal life or whole life insurance.

The insurance company collects its charges from your account, so if the mutual funds you've chosen increase significantly, increasing your account, you could stop paying premiums earlier. But if the market declines, you may have to pay higher premiums than initially anticipated. Therefore, you must choose the funds carefully.

Often, variable life offers a **fixed-account option,** which allows you to put some of your premium dollars into a fixed account with a guaranteed interest rate, backed by the insurance company's general assets. This fund is protected against declines in the stock market, and it's a good idea to put part of your premiums here to avoid having your entire account decline if the stock market falls.

◆ ◆ ◆

In whole life, universal life, and variable life insurance, part of your premium goes to pay for the costs of the insurance protection, and the remainder goes into your cash value. The difference between these three lies in their flexibility.

Of the three, whole life is the most rigid. You have to pay certain premiums. You may get a dividend determined by the insurance company. Guaranteed cash values grow slowly. Whole life also has some advantages, including the automatic savings plan it provides and its borrowing options. Its major disadvantage is its long-term, inflexible commitment.

In universal life, you can usually change your premium and death benefit, and you have an actual account to which interest is credited and charges are deducted. However, if you stop paying premiums and interest rates fall, you may have to put more premiums into the policy than you initially expected. So pay attention to the guaranteed values of any illustration you receive, and to any changes the insurance company makes to the interest rate or charges. As with whole life, you need to trust that the insurance company is investing your money wisely, but if you've picked a solid company and you like the additional flexibility, universal life may be for you.

Variable life provides the most flexibility, since you're choosing the mutual funds for your account. But it has several drawbacks. For one, the policies' fees tend to be higher. And the funds you've picked may decline, and with them the value of your account. In the case of a catastrophic decline, you may have to come up with more premiums at a time when other sources of money may be difficult to access; in other words, you may have to take money out of a mutual fund to pay your insurance premium, although the value of your mutual fund may have declined also. But if you're looking to hold on to your policy for a long time, and you have enough money so that you'll have the cash for premiums even in a severe decline in mutual fund values, then variable life may be for you.

◆ ◆ ◆

One other kind of life insurance worth mentioning here is **last survivor,** which insures two or more people, and pays a death benefit at the last death. Last survivor insurance is used most frequently to insure the lives of a married couple.

The advantage of last survivor involves estate taxes at the second death. When a spouse dies, the surviving spouse doesn't pay taxes. But when the second spouse dies, estate taxes (for the wealthy) can take more than half of your legacy. This type of insurance ensures that the beneficiaries will have more money left over after the government takes its share.

Why not buy an insurance policy for each spouse, where a death benefit will be paid on the individual's death? Because last survivor insurance is cheap. One last survivor policy for a million dollars is much cheaper than two individual policies for half a million.

Last survivor life insurance comes in many forms. It can be structured like a whole life policy, and pay dividends or have indeterminate premiums. It can look like a universal life policy, with a distinct account to which the insurance company credits interest and from which it deducts charges. Or it can resemble a variable life policy, where you choose how to invest your premium dollars.

Taxes can also be a factor in deciding what kind of insurance policy you want, and how you want to use it. Under current tax law, the increase in your cash value each year isn't taxable as long as you leave the money in the insurance policy. However, all insurance policies can be separated into two types: those where the withdrawal of cash values is subject to tax penalties, called **modified endowment contracts,** or MECs, and those not subject to tax penalties. If your contract is a MEC, withdrawals of cash, or using the policy's cash value as collateral, will incur a 10 percent penalty. The rules about withdrawing funds from MECs are similar to those governing early withdrawals from IRAs, so if you think you may need to withdraw some of your money, make sure the policy is not a MEC.

Death benefits from any life-insurance policy you buy on your own aren't income-taxable. So the beneficiaries of the policy won't have to declare the benefit as income on their 1040 form in April. However, the death benefit can end up in your estate, and as you can guess, the IRS loves to eat up pieces of your estate. The way to prevent this is to **irrevocably assign** the policy to the beneficiary, so that the beneficiary owns the policy, the death benefit, and any cash value. (We also talked a little about this in the estate-planning section.) But by doing this, you lose control over the policy. In addition, if you assign the policy to the beneficiary, the value of the policy at that time is subject to gift taxation. So you need to decide when you buy the policy what's best for you and for your heirs.

Here's one more insurance term that you've probably heard of but don't know much about: **annuities.** Although in some states they can be bought at banks, for the most part they come to you via your favorite insurance company.

An annuity is an investment that provides you with an income for as long as the policy states. This could be for ten years, twenty years, or the rest of your life, no matter how long you live.

The advantage of an annuity is that, like an IRA, your investment earnings are tax-deferred until the funds are withdrawn.

Annuities come in several types. **Immediate annuity** policies agree to pay you an income starting immediately. In general, once you pay your premium, you're locked into the contract. You have a guaranteed income and no future premiums, but you'll never be able to withdraw any of your premium. These aren't the best place for all your savings.

If you purchase a **life-only annuity,** payments are made throughout your life, and stop at your death. If you die in an accident driving home from your agent's office, having just picked up your immediate annuity policy, your poor heirs will receive nothing from the insurance company.

A **ten-year certain and life annuity** guarantees payments for ten years, whether or not you live that long, and more payments for as long as you remain alive. Thus Methuseleh would have received them for 969 years, if his company didn't go out of business paying him.

Immediate annuities can be **fixed** or **variable.**

Fixed immediate annuities pay you the same income every year, regardless of inflation.

A variable immediate annuity invests your money in mutual funds, as in variable life insurance. Your income increases or decreases over time with the value of the mutual funds.

Historically, mutual funds have surpassed inflation over the long term, but not year to year. So over time, you probably won't lose purchasing power with a variable immediate annuity, but you may lose purchasing power over the short term. And since the income in a fixed immediate annuity never changes, as long as inflation exists, you *will* lose purchasing power. So immediate annuities, whether fixed or variable, are best used to supplement your income, not to provide your total income.

Deferred annuities won't begin to pay you an income until some point in the future. When you buy the policy, you designate when you want to begin receiving your income.

Generally, deferred annuities also fall into the same fixed or variable category as above.

Annuities give you an income for the rest of your life, and you won't have to pay tax on the growth in your account until you make withdrawals. But there's a down side, besides the fact that, like as with an IRA, if you withdraw the money before you're 59$^{1}/_{2}$, you pay tax penalties. Annuity sales charges and fees can be high, and you have to watch out for fine print—sometimes the "locked-in" interest rates that agents might crow about aren't locked in at all. And remember that your money isn't insured: Unlike as with a savings bank, there's only limited protection for you if your company goes under. Given all the choices for investing money today, annuities are not as popular as they once were.

And now, if you've read through all this information, and you've understood it fully, and you want to know still more, you might want to consider a new career. There's always a job available for an insurance agent.

Financial Index

life insurance (*cont.*)
   estate taxes and, 94, 106, 195, 196
   last survivor, 195–96
   premiums in, 189, 190, 191, 192,
      194, 195
   taxes and, 196
   term, 51, 189, 190–91
   whole, 51, 191–92, 194
life-only annuities, 197
lifetime exemption, 88, 90
liquid assets, 123
living trusts, 93, 151–52
living wills, 97
load funds, 138–39
long-term care insurance, 109–10

margin, buying on, 145
marital deduction in estate taxes, 88–89
market risk, 125, 131
MECs (modified endowment
    contracts), 196
medical expenses as tax deductions,
    75
Medicare, 17, 109, 169
Medigap insurance, 170
modified endowment contracts
    (MECs), 196
money management accounts,
    brokerage accounts vs., 141
money market accounts, 124, 134
municipal bonds, 67, 81
mutual funds, 37, 136–39, 181
   asset allocation in, 137–38
   buying of, 137, 138
   expenses in, 138
   load vs. no-load, 138–39

net asset value, 136–37, 138
no-load funds, 138

open-end funds, 137

pension plans:
   income tax and, 74, 87–88
   1997 tax bill and, 168
   taxes on, 88
personal liability insurance, 106,
    112
policy loans, 189
portfolios:
   asset allocation in, 135
   monitoring of, 147
power of attorney, 93, 97
preferred provider organization
    (PPO), 108, 109
preferred stock, 132
premiums, life insurance, 189
   in term insurance, 190
   in universal life, 192, 195
   in variable life, 194
   in whole life insurance, 191
probate, 91, 93
professional liability insurance, 106,
    112
property, community, 85, 86
prospectus, 136

qualified terminable interest property
    trust (QTIP), 91–92

retirement:
   health insurance in, 169–70
   lifestyle in, 165–66
retirement pension plans, 167–69
   401(k), 78, 167, 168
   403(b), 167, 168
   IRAs, 66–67, 78, 167, 168
   Keogh, 78, 167, 168
   SEPs, 167, 168–69
   women and, 161–62

umbrella insurance policies, 112, 152
universal life insurance, 192–93, 195
  illustration of values in, 192

values, in universal life insurance,
  192–93
variable annuities, 197
variable life insurance, 193–94
  fixed-account option of, 194
  flexibility of, 195
  premiums in, 194

whole-life insurance, 51, 191–
  192
  inflexibility of, 194
  participating policies in, 191
  premiums in, 191
wills, 17, 85
  cost of, 96
  executors of, 98
  holographic, 96–97
  living, 97
  storage of, 96